With Hands Outstretched

by Donald L. Adams

With Hands Outstretched
©Donald L. Adams
Published by Bristol House, Ltd.

First Printing, May 2008

ISBN: 978-1-885224-60-6
Printed in the United States of America.

BRISTOL HOUSE, LTD.
1201 E. 5th St., Suite 2107
Anderson, Indiana 46012
Phone: 765-644-0856
Fax: 765-622-1045

To order call: 1-800-451-READ (7323)
www.bristolhouseltd.com

CONTENTS

Preface

The greatest service that anyone can do for another is to point clearly toward Christ Jesus, who is Lord and Savior for the whole world. This is the central affirmation of the Apostolic Church, and it is exclaimed in praise and worship each and every Lord's Day in many languages and cultures all over the world.

This book is a great gift to everyone who reads it. It is a study about life and what matters most in life. As you read the biblical text and utilize the guide offered by the author, you find yourself stretching out your hands to receive the gift of grace and truth offered from God the Father in Jesus Christ, Lord and Savior. A deep craving in the human heart is to know meaning and fulfillment in life. Don Adams has a way of enabling one to feel that this letter of the apostle Paul is written as a personal letter to each one of us. Through his own experiences and testimony, we are introduced to the living presence of Jesus Christ in the now.

It is has been my privilege to be in worship experiences with Christians all over the world. As I hear people sing in different languages, it is always a moving moment when I hear a tune that is familiar. There is one hymn that in my experience is always sung to the same tune. It is the words of the hymn, "What a friend we have in Jesus, all our sins and grief to bear...." Everywhere I have been in the world the people know this hymn. The simple words link together people in many cultures and circumstances, for it points to the relationship with the friend of friends, Jesus the Christ. In the author's unique expression, we are invited to experience the relationship in the "Person-driven life."

The letter to the Philippians is clear. Christian faith is not a generic faith; it is a centered faith in Christ Jesus, Lord of Creation, Lord of History, and Savior for the whole world.

On my desk I keep a small, broken piece from the Berlin Wall. I recall the time when this wall separated a people from one another. I remember gathering in a prayer meeting with Christians near the east side of the wall and praying that the walls which divide people would come tumbling down. Following the prayer meeting in the east, we traveled through "Checkpoint Charlie" to the other side. Again, we gathered with Christians and prayed the same prayers for the wall to come "tumbling down." And by the grace of God, the wall which divided the people does not have the last word!

This is the powerful message in this letter. The apostle Paul's testimony reminds us that there is a power which overcomes evil and opens up the fullness of life here and in the world to come.

As we read again the letter to the Philippians, we find ourselves joining with the early church in singing this hymn of unending praise:

Therefore God also highly exalted him
And gave him the name that is above every name,
So that at the name of Jesus every knee should bend,
In heaven and on earth and under the earth,
And every tongue should confess
That Jesus Christ is Lord, to the glory of God the Father.

Philippians 2:9-11

We commend this excellent Bible study to you and pray that it will enable you to experience a deeper relationship in Christ Jesus. My good friend, Don Adams, invites us to reach out to receive the incredible gift of grace and salvation that is in Christ Jesus. The "Person-driven life" is one of joy and fulfillment. Let us study *With Hands Outstretched*.

H. Eddie Fox
World Director of Evangelism
World Methodist Council

Introduction

My ears perk up when Jesus uses the word *never.*

"Unless you become like a child you will *never* [my emphasis] enter the kingdom of heaven." It sounds as though we ought to know what it means to "become like a child," doesn't it? At one time my answer would have sounded like a college essay, but that was before rearing four children.

As it turned out, the answer was obviously simple and simply obvious. Becoming like a child means embracing the fact that we are in a parent-child relationship with God, and *God is the Parent.*

Years ago I was in Madison, Wisconsin, to be trained to lead the *Bethel Bible Series,* granddaddy of the "through the Bible" studies. The creator of that material, Harley Swiggum, was teaching from the early chapters of Genesis. He was the first person in my hearing to make the comparison of the first Adam with the second Adam, Jesus, on the basis of Philippians 2.

The first Adam in the Genesis narrative had wanted to be his own parent (in this case, God), and the result was disastrous. In an absolute reversal of attitude, Jesus, the second Adam, *was* God and chose to empty himself of the rights and privileges thereof. The outcome of these two diametrically opposed attitudes was decisively clear. Adam rejected "becoming like a child," while Jesus embraced it.

Here was the panorama of the Bible and life, mine included, reduced to two snapshots. One was a picture of humankind seeking to be God-like, *losing life by grasping at it.* The other picture was that of true humanity, not empty of self, but emptied of the clutching at God-ness that cost our ancient parents paradise. The contrast was as sharp as pink neon against black. I saw as never before the primal wisdom and grace of Jesus: He lived as we were intended to live, empty of designs on deity, daily seeking not divine rights, but divine fellowship and leadership. Put simply, he lived like a child, always in relationship to his Father.

Since that moment I have been drawn as by a powerful spiritual magnet to Paul's letter to the Philippians. It is here, in the everyday terms of a pastor to his people, that can be found the heartbeat of life. The Christ hymn of chapter two is where the heartbeat of the letter is strongest. Offering no explanation of how God became one of us, these brief words nonetheless throb with the power of Christ more profoundly than a library of theology books.

This reminds me of an anecdote told of Albert Einstein. He was asked to explain the theory of relativity. Picking up his violin, he responded, "I can't explain it, but I can play it for you." How do we explain the Incarnation, God Almighty taking the form of a servant, God Almighty becoming like a child? In a sense Paul says that he can't explain Jesus, but he can sing of his greatness! Philippians is a joyful theme and variation of that great song.

Rejoicing at the faith of the Philippians, Paul encourages this congregation he loved to live as the Savior lived—full of the gifts of grace and truth, empty of the reach for power and control that has cost humanity its birthright. Philippians is often spoken of as the "epistle of joy." I prefer to think of it as the epistle of a second childhood, a relationship with the Father that renews the joy of life that is commonly lost in the human grasp for control.

As this letter has become a part of my life, an image has appeared in my mind. It comes into clear focus in 3:13 where Paul writes,

> . . . my brothers, I do not consider myself to have fully grasped it even now. But I do concentrate on this: I leave the past behind and with hands outstretched to whatever lies ahead I go straight for the goal—my reward the honor of being called by God in Christ (J. B. Phillips).

"With hands outstretched . . ." What a simple image! What a human posture! Outstretched hands are empty, hopeful, ready. Outstretched hands are looking for the Parent whose hands they were intended to hold. Philippians is a letter encouraging us to be children who reach for the Father who, in turn, is already reaching for us through Jesus Christ. When Paul affirms, "For me to live is Christ" (1:21), he identifies himself as Person-driven, a willing servant of the One at whose name every knee will one day bow.

Understanding faith to be the spiritual hands with which we, as children, receive the gifts of God that they might be shared with the world, let us journey with Paul to Philippi, with hands outstretched!

CHAPTER ONE

Christianity Is a Team Sport
(We Are Made for Relationships)

Philippians 1:1-2
Paul and Timothy, servants of Christ Jesus.
To all the saints in Christ Jesus at Philippi,
together with the overseers and deacons . . . .

What is the most common temptation? Is it sexual? Does it have to do with greed or ambition? Are we most often tempted to judge others? These are all common. But they are not the most common. The most common temptation is the gnawing urge to quit, to feel in control by pulling inward. The original sin grew out of the desire to quit obeying the Creator, to quit being obedient children. Inherent in the urge to quit is an inner force that wants to push us away from having to deal with real life, with real people, with the real God, and with our true self. It can be helpful when we experience any kind of temptation, if we can gather the presence of mind to do it, to ask the questions, "What or whom is this desire trying to push me away from?" and "In what way does this temptation satisfy my need for control?"

The apostle Paul had wrestled with this same primal push. We read in Romans 7 of his inner battles with things he shouldn't do and things he should but didn't want to do. His experience reflects the irony that the things we do attempting to feel more in control are the very things that ultimately lead to a feeling of being out of control. In that same portion of Romans, Paul goes on to say that there is an antidote for this problem. "Who will rescue me from this body of death? Thanks be to God—through Jesus Christ our Lord!" (7:24-25)

In Jesus Christ, God has acted in a new and living way to provide a righteous, loving, and gracious response to the original drive, which repels us from abundant life. In Philippians Paul will express this in different ways.

God "began a good work in you" (1:6)
"righteousness that comes through Jesus Christ" (1:11)
"to me, to live is Christ" (1:21)
"united with Christ" (2:1)
"it is God who works in you" (2:13)
"I want to know Christ" (3:10)
"Christ Jesus took hold of me" (3:12)
"him who gives me strength" (4:13)
"his glorious riches in Christ Jesus" (4:19)

All of these speak of the divine initiative in Jesus that has revealed the nature of righteousness, provided a conclusive act of atonement and unleashed the power of God in a way that "all flesh" can receive the desire and the enabling to live as children of God. These are resources that help us overcome the pull inward, to have freedom to move toward righteous love and truth, to desire to draw near to God without fear and to "have the mind of Christ," which is to be motivated by loving obedience rather than anxiety. These resources have their nexus in Jesus Christ, a living Presence in whom believers may abide to live fruitful, child-of-God lives.

Immediately there is a hint of this power to overcome the inward pull at work in the first three words of this letter, "Paul and Timothy."

Now consider this: What would it mean to you if a letter such as this began, "Paul and [*your name*]"?

It would dramatically alter the significance of every sentence, wouldn't it? You would be thrust into a world of life-altering relationships. Those relationships would become lenses through which everything would look different.

And this is exactly the way that the Christian life, being in Christ, is supposed to affect us.

Our walk of faith is intended to be an immersion into new dimensions of relationships with God and others called the kingdom of God. Methodist missionary and widely read author E. Stanley Jones was known to say that the kingdom of God is the kingdom of right relationships. On the throne of this kingdom is One who came to relate. Pause for a moment and ask yourself these questions:

- Do I realize that "the Word became flesh" was not coincidental to the reason Jesus came, but absolutely central?
- Are relationships with others essential to my Christian faith, or just coincidental with my pursuit of spiritual satisfaction?
- What relationships are a direct result of my faith?

"Paul and Timothy. . . ." This salutation makes it clear that Paul believed that relationships—encouraging, time-consuming, enlightening, energy-draining, life-saving and sometimes painful —are central to the Christian faith. Do you?

What might have the Philippian congregation inferred from this salutation?

Paul was willing to take the time to disciple others.

Paul was willing to share the "glory" of leadership.

Paul was willing to identify with others who were weaker in the faith.

Paul was willing to empower younger people.

Paul's faith was more than "Jesus and me."

We know that Paul struggled with some of his relationships, such as with Mark and Barnabas, as well as with other people in the churches he began. So what prompted him to value relationships?

It was the example and teachings of Jesus.

Being in Christ, having the mind of Christ, knowing the glorious liberty of the children of God (Romans 8:21), is not found in isolationist piety. It prospers in the environment of relationships, with God, with others.

A Healthy Human Being is a Person in Relationships

Why did Jesus place such tremendous importance on maintaining relationships through the forgiving of others? Why would he go so far as to say that we risk forfeiting our own forgiveness if we are unwilling to extend it to those who sin against us? According to God relationships are essential to human life. We are made in the image of a triune God, a God whom we understand as three Persons in one. While this is a profound mystery, it would seem to indicate inter-relationships within the Creator. This is not an esoteric reality. To the contrary, it provides the greatest possible affirmation to the crucial significance of relationships as part and parcel of our very souls.

The ancient story of Cain and Abel illustrates the intrinsic link between the soul and relationships. When Cain's relationship with God was strained, his relationship with his brother was equally unhealthful. Reading this story from Genesis 4 we initially think that God had a problem with the content of Cain's offerings, and consequently God rejected them. The composition of his offerings was secondary. It was Cain's heart that mattered, and his heart was far from God. As a consequence, his heart was *also* far from his brother. So, God could not accept what Cain offered. The condition of his heart directly affected his relationships and vice versa. Murdering Abel was the shattering result of living in a spirit of autonomy. Our rebellion against God manifests itself in rebellion against our neighbor. What does your attitude toward your neighbor tell you about your relationship with God?

Paul and Timothy

While serving in a certain community, I became acquainted

with someone completely absorbed in a New Age religion. This worldview sees all people as perfect. According to this perspective, everyone simply needs to embrace his inherent perfection. That seemed crazy to me. But I got to know the person better, seeing more clearly her wounded heart. In a tangential way, the truth of French mathematician and philosopher Pascal's saying, "the heart has reasons that reason knows nothing of," made rational what was otherwise irrational. Following such a religion, adherents never have to deal with the pain of broken relationships, including the most basic relationship of all, with our Creator. The only thing for which one might need to be forgiven was failing to realize one's perfection.

Christians must be aware of bending their faith to avoid the pain of relationships, being too individualistic or judgmental. As a pastor I am highly sensitive to the inner struggles, often the result of scars from former relationships, that people bring to their faith life. It is precisely because of pastoral concerns that I guide believers to lean into the pain (as priest/author Henri Nouwen put it) that relationships bring to the surface. We pastors wrestle with the same temptation to drop out when relationships seem to wound rather than bless. If I had a dollar for every time I have wanted to quit because of a painful relationship. . . well, you know.

At such times we can retreat into a relationship mode akin to the old diving-bell suit. We have our own spiritual lifeline that reaches above to the Savior. We don't need others. This inclination among super-spiritual Methodists led John Wesley to affirm that the only real Christianity was, in his term, "social" Christianity. A little logic affirms his position. Jesus taught that the greatest commandment was to love God with all of oneself. Then he added that there was another commandment of similar consequence: love your neighbor as yourself. Unilateral Christianity is an oxymoron that lives in denial of the high calling of love as Jesus lived it and taught it (Matthew 22:37-39). It is a surrender to the centrifugal force of sin that pushes people apart.

As a pastor of thirty-plus years and a supervisor of dozens of churches, I can assure you that it does not take a rocket scientist to figure out what gnaws at the heart of many declining congregations. It is people who don't know how or are unwilling to love their neighbor in the context of a faith community. We sometimes call the most challenging of such people "controllers," or as church consultant Paul Borden describes them, "emotional terrorists." These are not team players. Controllers usually wrestle for influence with congregational leadership. At the heart of their pathology is a blindness to what real leadership, which is never unilateral, means.

Paul's correspondence reflects an individual involved in community and shared ministry. Even in prison he rejoices at those who have steadfastly remained with him. Barnabas, Silas, Timothy and Luke were real people with whom Paul worked out his salvation in fear and trembling. Paul was a leader, not a manager, not a controller.

In the final chapter of Acts one reads an understated but moving scene as Paul draws near to Rome and the likely end of his earthly life. Luke is with him. They anticipate meeting some of the Christians who lived in that hub of the ancient world. Paul had corresponded with these believers, but had never seen them face to face. Now, 40 miles from Rome, they have their first meeting. Acts 28:15 tells us, "The brothers there had heard that we were coming and they traveled as far as the Forum of Appius and the Three Taverns to meet us." These friends in Christ walked 40 miles to greet him and accompany him back to whatever awaited him in Rome. Luke tells us, "At the sight of these men Paul thanked God and was encouraged." The great Bible expositor, John R. Stott, explains it this way:

> One sometimes meets super-spiritual people
> who claim that they never feel lonely and have
> no need of human friends.

> But human friendship is the loving provision
> of God for mankind.
>   It was God himself who said in the beginning:
> "it is not good that man should be alone" (Gen.
> 2:18). Wonderful as are both the presence of
> the Lord Jesus every day and the prospect of his
> coming on the last day, they are not intended to
> be a substitute for human friendship (*Guard the
> Gospel,* p. 120).

Paul, though he had experienced pain in the church, did not shun relationships. He was not a spiritual Lone Ranger. This need for others was put in the heart by the Creator. Those who consider themselves too spiritual to need earthly friends should check themselves for an overload of fear, anger, guilt or a Grinch-sized heart.

One of the towering figures of the Bible is also one who modeled a wonderful friendship. David, Israel's greatest king, was a person acquainted with the power and blessing of a friend. His relationship with Jonathan is captured in the words of I Samuel 18:1, ". . . Jonathan became one in spirit with David, and he loved him as himself." In the heat of David's struggle with Jonathan's father, King Saul, we observe one of friendship's most magnificent purposes: "And Saul's son Jonathan went to David at Horesh, and helped him find strength in God" (I Samuel 23:16).

Like the apostle Paul centuries later, David found courage to go on through the bond of friendship, a gift springing from the very nature of God.

Paul and Timothy

Any pastor who has weathered a time of conflict in the church knows how precious true friends can be, those who help you find strength in God. Enduring such a period in ministry, I was awakened early one Saturday morning by the telephone. It was a layman from a nearby community, a man I had known for several years. In his prayers that morning he had felt a burden for me. He asked if he could come over.

Sitting in our living room, he read Scripture and prayed for my wife and me. When he left I felt like singing, "What a Friend We Have in Wesley" (our friend's name). Brenda and I knew Jesus had sent him to us, and that was enough. We not only found strength, but we knew also that Strength had found us. Our hands had been outstretched to God in prayer for many months. What a difference to sense our Lord's hands reaching out to us through a praying friend.

In his 1973 book *The Becomers*, Keith Miller quotes psychiatrist Jean Rosenbaum who had written, "Chronic loneliness affects 75-90% of all Americans." I have no reason to think her figures excluded Christians. In our "high tech-low touch" society, have things become better in this regard since 1973?

A Healthy Christian Reaches out to Others

It is not good for people to be alone. This is not God's design. Like David and Paul we not only need friends to give us courage, but we also need to be friends to others.

It is intriguing that things often hide in plain sight. I am convinced that one such thing is the wonderful ministry of simply being friendly. If there was a volume knob on this page I would turn it up and loudly declare, "You can have a profound ministry just by being friendly!" This is especially true in the context of the church where friendship has the support of community, teaching, worship, and service.

At worship services, in Sunday school classes, at fellowship suppers I have watched newcomers or shy people enter the room. None has ever worn a sign reading "Unclean!" Yet again and again, as though they were wearing a scarlet letter, people are left to fade awkwardly into the woodwork. I can understand the person who says, "My gifts are not up front, like speaking or teaching or leading meetings. Please don't ask me to do those sorts of things." (I do not always listen to that, of course.) But is it too much to expect folks to say, "Hello, my name is Joe. Glad you are here"? It is hard to overestimate the value of this admittedly superficial, but foundational step in ministry.

From opening the door of relationships that begins with friendliness, a further step can lead to enabling others literally to bond (or not bond) with the fellowship of the church. Church growth authority Winn Arn noted the significance of what he termed the "friendship ratio." As new people come into the life of a church they should be able to identify at least seven friends within the congregation in six months. He observes, "Friendship appears to be the strongest bond cementing new members to their congregation" (*Leadership*, Sp. '84, p. 29).

Did you hear that? It is not preaching or teaching or programs, but friendship! And what happens to people who do not enter into a network of friendships? Within six months they are likely to head out the "back door" of the church. In his book, *Practicing the Presence of People*, author Mike Mason writes:

> Over the centuries many spiritual books have been written on love, but little has been written on friendship. The reason, I believe, is that church people generally know little about it. Compared to such great concerns as sound doctrine, evangelism, prayer, worship, and ministry, friendship does not seem so important. But the truth is that friendship is the foundation for all the rest. Without it the church will never accomplish her mission on earth (pp. 242-43).

If we want a church that makes disciples, the prescription is clear. We must be a church that makes friends! Christian believers not only need friends, but need to *be* friends. Wanting friends is a God-created need. Being a friend is a God-given opportunity. The mind of Christ is an attitude that is much more likely to build bridges than to blow them up.

Charles Kingsley once wrote, "If you wish to be miserable, you must think about yourself; about what you want, what you like, what respect people ought to pay you, and then to you nothing will be pure. You will spoil everything God sends you. You can be as wretched as you choose" (*The Art of Understanding Yourself*, C. Osborne, p.9).

Martin Luther, 400 years ago, defined sin as "the heart curled up inside itself." God, in making us helpmates to one other, has made us want to befriend each other, to stretch out our hands to the person standing beside us. As such, friendship becomes more than a gratifying relationship with someone of like-mind or temperament. It is transformed into an opportunity to "love at all times," as the proverb says. It becomes a source of spiritual therapy in uncurling the heart.

Charles Swindoll, pastor and author, tells of an encounter with an old Marine buddy who, during their enlisted days, was as profane and carnal as they come. In later years this man met Jesus Christ. As they reminisced, the old friend said, "Chuck, the only thing I miss is that old fellowship that all the guys in our outfit used to have down at the slop shoot (Greek for tavern on base). Man, we'd sit around, laugh, tell stories, drink a few beers, and really let our hair down. It was great! I just haven't found anything to take the place of that great time we used to enjoy. I ain't got nobody to admit my faults to . . . to have 'em put their arms around me and tell me I'm still okay" (*Encourage Me*, p. 18).

It sounds as though he was looking for the body of Christ, for a living church. It's easy to say, "Well, those kinds of relationships happen under the unique pressures of wartime, but not everyday life." Yes, you're right. What we must understand is that a war is on— a war against loneliness and fear and all the other results of hearts curled up within themselves. A friend of mine who is developing a ministry to men tells me that it is not uncommon for many men to have no close friends. In the excellent study of male life, *The Quest For Authentic Manhood*, pastor/teacher/author Robert Lewis includes a lesson entitled "The All Alone Wound." Listening to that teaching I couldn't help but connect the difficulty men often have in relating to God with our difficulty in forming deep relationships with anyone. In view of the pace at which we live, we might wonder if this is not increasingly true for women as well.

Author and seminary professor Dr. Leonard Sweet, in his book *Quantum Spirituality*, makes a strong case for the importance of touching in our culture. The "high-tech, low-touch" society to which I alluded earlier is desperately in need of wholesome personal contact between people. Dr. Sweet notes that the church has always included human touch in its congregational life—laying on of hands, baptism, ordination, foot washing and the "Holy Kiss."

Years ago I remember a fine but somewhat stiff seminary professor complaining about the "time of greeting" or "passing the peace" in corporate worship. He believed it was out of place. In today's world it is crucial. Yes, it can be superficial (thankfully we haven't let that possibility stop worship altogether). But it can also help break down the barriers that exist between people who otherwise sit passively and stare at the hairdo in front of them. In a day of "drive-through" funeral homes and "900 numbers" offering "companionship," I agree with Dr. Sweet when he writes, "There are not enough 'touch me' congregations in this hands off…culture" (p. 33).

As Christians together, we can provide the arena for personal contact, confession and restoration with those who participate in the life of the church. At the same time we must stay in circulation beyond our fellowship walls where the war with loneliness is likely at its worst.

- Where single parents struggle with loneliness (not living with anyone on their level of consciousness), finances, parenting and working;
- Where adolescents are bombarded with the napalm of temptation, often via so-called "friends";
- Where marriages are under the pressures of a society that does not

know how to let the heat of marital differences forge real love in a relationship;
• Where children are allowed (and often encouraged) to look and act like adults before their emotional wiring can stand the voltage;
• Where business people often find that personal relationships are the first thing thrown overboard when profits lag;
• Where sub-cultures build more walls than bridges.

It is in such a world that friendship is needed and can become the cup of cold water given in Jesus' name. William Barclay, the beloved Bible commentator, was right on when he wrote,

> One of the highest of human duties is the duty of encouragement.
> It is easy to laugh at men's ideals; it is easy to pour cold water on their enthusiasm; it is easy to discourage others. The world is full of discouragers. We have a Christian duty to encourage one another. Many a time a word of praise or thanks or appreciation or cheer has kept a man on his feet. Blessed is the man who speaks such a word (*Encourage Me*, p. 48).

As Christians, we are especially called to befriend the friendless. We remember Jesus' words, "In as much as you have done it unto the least of these, my brothers, you have done it unto me" (Matthew 25:40).

Years ago as a teenager living near Indianapolis, I remember a new anchorman coming to one of the network affiliates in that city. The local station trumpeted him as a real catch. His first broadcast was eagerly awaited. As he made his introductory remarks, he looked into the camera with confidence and assurance. I still remember his saying, "In this business, some people cut the baloney pretty thick," the implication being that he would not. My recollection is that he lasted about a year and moved on.

As I discuss being friendly to the friendless, it is my heartfelt desire not to cut the baloney thick. This is a prime place to say easily, "Lord, Lord," and not do what he says (Matthew 7:21). I suspect many people would identify with my own struggle with busyness in the Lord's work, busyness that is generally related to the institution of the church. How alarmingly possible it is to "give your body to be burned" for the church and not have love. People involved in church growth use the term "redemption and lift" to refer to the reality that new Christians tend to leave old circles of relationships behind as they bond with new friends in Christ. Opportunities for outreach are left behind.

Across the years of my own life as a Christian, I can discern no pattern to the way "opportunities" for love in Jesus' name have come forth. They have all been wrapped in different faces and needs. Ultimately, in each instance, one common denominator has surfaced. That common denominator is captured in a true story Tony Campolo tells of a boy who endured the agonies of Nazi Germany during World War II. This Jewish boy lived in a small Polish village, the Jewish citizens of which were rounded up by Nazi SS troops for execution. The boy and his neighbors were forced to work together to dig a shallow ditch for their graves. Then they were lined up and gunned down. Their dead bodies fell into the ditch where a shallow covering of dirt sufficed for burial. Amazingly enough the boy was not hit by the bullets. His naked body was splattered with the blood of his parents. As they fell, lifeless into the ditch, he fell upon them, pretending to be dead. The shallow covering of earth allowed him to breathe until darkness fell and he could claw his way out of the grave.

With blood and dirt caked to his body, he found his way to the nearest house. When the door opened and he was recognized as one of those marked for death by the SS, the door was promptly slammed in his face. Again and again the fear of the Nazis overpowered any possible compassion as home after home was closed to him. Then a thought found its way into his mind, leading him to say something different at the next door to which he came. When the family responded to his timid knocking, they heard him say, "Don't you recognize me? I am the Jesus you say you love." There was a long pause. Then the woman of the house swept the boy up in her arms and took him in. From that point forward he became a part of that family (*Who Switched the Price Tags*, pp. 119-20).

The common denominator for those whom we might befriend is simple: They are very likely Jesus waiting to be welcomed. Yes, I realize this sounds as if it could result in a kind of spiritual condescension where we say we are Christian enough to see Jesus in our needy neighbor. You know what? I don't care how it sounds! And I think the Lord doesn't care either. I believe Jesus offered us this way of seeing others because he knows that we are selfish sinners and we need help in overcoming ourselves.

Some years ago I found myself in a hostile attitude toward a child in our neighborhood. He bugged me! No matter how hard I tried, he always brought out negative feelings in me. Then one day I remembered the story of the Jewish boy looking for help. I could almost hear his words, "Don't you recognize me? I am the Jesus you say you love," coming out of the mouth of my little neighbor. It made an immediate difference in my attitude. Grace had been turned loose. Rather than feeling holy that I was so spiritual and able to see Jesus in this child, I was humbled that my own selfishness was so entrenched it took such a measure to break me free. I certainly felt no superiority to that child. Rather, I was reminded of the depth of my own need.

The principle on which this was first built found its way into my life years ago when I heard E. Stanley Jones speak. Although I didn't fully grasp the implication of it at the time, I was impressed to write these words inside the cover of my Bible: "It is easier to act your way into a feeling than to feel your way into an action." He was saying that as Christians we cannot wait for the right feelings before we act. We must do what is right and realize that the feelings usually will follow.

I have known Christians who felt themselves to be hypocritical if they acted loving when they didn't feel like it. This is thinking "as men think and not as God thinks." We must not limit our friendships to those with whom we have "good vibrations." Even the pagans do that.

Paul and Timothy

In one community where we served, a young man came to our church several Sundays. As we became acquainted I realized that there was deep anger and hostility in him from his childhood. When he quit coming to church I continued to visit him, wanting to be a friend in Christ to him. One day he sent me an expression of his frustration with our church. This is part of what he wrote.

Who Am I?

I'm the Christian you sat next to one Sunday, you must remember me.

The one you smiled at to show the warmth of the church.

The one you never spoke to.

The outsider, not belonging to your inner circle of friends.

What ever happened to Christian love, fellowship, or the invite to one's own home?

Is this a privilege only considered within one's own inner circle? How long since an outsider penetrated the wall of your inner circle? One month, two, maybe six months or more.

I'm the new guy you've smiled at many times, welcomed to your church maybe three times. Your responsibility ends there, after all someone else will fill the responsibility of being my friend . . . .

My heart yearned for Christian fellowship. . .my prayers were for a friend. . .the friend who never revealed his/herself. . .

Where did I go?

You obviously didn't care since you haven't called.

Maybe I was killed in an auto accident; maybe I committed suicide.

But it doesn't matter—your inner circle of friends wasn't disturbed.

We in the church could offer a defense against these accusations. We could analyze the anger and biases revealed by his judgments. But such protests miss the point, which is that there are many, many people in our midst who are profoundly lonely and hurting. They see Christians as "relational millionaires," rich in fellowship, but holding onto what they have lest anyone take it away. They challenge us to lift up our eyes and see the fields that are ready to harvest, full of aching hearts. We need to see friendship as a vital opportunity to love others as the Lord would do.

(Another challenging angle on the ministry of friendship is in the broad area of hospitality as a Christian behavior. Two books that can introduce this subject from academic and pastoral viewpoints are *Making Room: Recovering Hospitality As a Christian Tradition* by Christine Pohl and *Widening the Welcome of Your Church: Hospitality & the Vital Congregation* by Fred Bernhard. Such studies strongly affirm the ancient place of "welcoming the stranger" in the Christian tradition.)

A Healthy Christian Knows the Greatest Friend of All

Not only do we need friends and need to be a friend, but we also have the ultimate friend in Jesus Christ.

Christian pastor, author and philosopher Francis Schaefer once observed with true spiritual wisdom that we tend to expect too much from our personal relationships; they cannot bear the weight. He reminds us that all people are sinful, flawed and incomplete. He says, ". . . when I acknowledge that none of us are perfect in this life, I can enjoy that which is beautiful in a relationship without expecting it to be perfect" (*True Spirituality*, p. 152).

Such wisdom is needed when it comes to being a friend or having friends. There is only one friendship that can carry the weight of our deepest longings through the years— it is our friendship with God by God's Spirit through his Son. Leslie Weatherhead, English author and pastor, writes in *The Transforming Friendship* that the essence of the Christian faith can be boiled down to one thought: accepting the gift of friendship with Jesus. He suggests that the greatest difficulty of being a Christian is not intellectual, but a matter of simply being loyal to the Lord who calls his church his friends.

While no single image, including friendship, can reflect all of the dimensions of Christianity, this viewpoint does offer insight in a couple of ways. It helps us see that Christian faith begins with the acceptance of a gift and that it is a personal relationship at its heart.

Some years ago in the Bowery section of New York City a teenager was spotted on the ledge of a high building about to jump. Soon a crowd gathered. Chants of "jump, jump, jump" came from the onlookers gathered below.

A veteran policeman was called in and for more than an hour he talked with the young man. At last the teenager came down, and the policeman walked beside him with his arm draped around his shoulder. The crowd jeered, having missed their thrill.

A month later a television station from another city sent a reporter to New York to interview the young man as a follow-up to the story. They asked him, "Why did you come down from the ledge?" He answered, "I listened to what the policeman said, and I listened to the mob below, telling me to jump. I thought to myself, 'This is New York. This is where I was going to make it. But New York is telling me to jump.' I was about to jump. All of a sudden the policeman said to me, 'You know, I wouldn't mind having you for a son.' That blew my mind. No one had ever wanted me—not my father, my mother, or any relative. I looked and he seemed to mean it."

As the young man continued, he explained how the policeman actually followed through on what he said. He literally adopted the boy ("Friends and Friendship," a sermon by David Seamands).

Is not this the Christian faith at work? Through Jesus Christ, the Father says to us, "I wouldn't mind having you for a son, a daughter." Jesus, by his grace, says to us, "I wouldn't mind having you for a friend." This is the ultimate friendship of life and is available to anyone who will receive it. The mind of Christ in us will help us overcome the fears that subtly and not so subtly push us away from one another.

Friendship is a costly thing, isn't it? Sometimes we do not want to pay the price. Yet, there is something about having a real friend that encourages us to want to be of a like spirit. Everyone has such a friend in Jesus. Later in Philippians Paul will remind us of the price that Christ paid in order to be our friend. Just as he emptied himself of his rights as heavenly royalty, so he encourages us to lay aside our ego and make room for others in our lives.

"Paul and Timothy" what power their friendship unleashed. It was the power of the kingdom to pull people together, given to those who become like children.

Occasionally people ask if there is any secret to a successful Christian life and a vital Christian church. Don't quit being *friends* with one another, *friends* to the friendless and *friends* with Jesus. Friendship is often where it all begins. So it is with this letter to the people of Philippi.

Questions for Discussion

1. Martin Luther would ask his companions in spiritual formation, "Where have your temptations lead you?" What have you learned about yourself through your temptations?

2. New Testament scholar Robert Mulholland has defined spiritual formation as "the process of being conformed to the image of God for the sake of others." Why did he define growth in discipleship as taking place for the sake of others?

3. Why does "the flesh" often pull us away from healthy relationships with others?

4. At this point in your life, how does your relationship with God influence/affect your relationships with others (see I John 4:20-21)?

5. What is the difference between management and leadership? What is the place of each in the church? In a family?

6. Does the concept of the "friendship ratio" seem accurate to you? What can Christians do to turn this phenomenon into a plan of action?

7. What do you think about the "passing of the peace" or a "time of greeting" as a part of Sunday morning worship? What is the theological rationale for such a practice? How could it be made more meaningful?

8. What does it mean for your coworker or neighbor or someone you do not care about to be "the Jesus you say you love"?

9. In seeking to be obedient to God have you ever "acted your way into a feeling"? Explain. Is it hypocritical to act as a Christian before we feel like it? Why or why not?

10. How do we enjoy relationships without expecting them to be perfect?

CHAPTER TWO

Grace: The Surprise We Must Never Get Over
(We Are Saved By Grace.)

Philippians 1:2
Grace and peace to you from God the Father and the Lord Jesus Christ.

A seasoned citizen decided it was time to make his "final arrangements." Sitting in a funeral home office he responded as the funeral director read off a checklist of issues. Near the top of the sheet was a fundamental question: "Do you desire a traditional burial or do you wish to be cremated?" The elderly gentleman thought for a moment and then piped up, "Surprise me!"

Paul knew what it meant to be surprised. Self-righteously steaming along the Damascus Road he experienced a totally unanticipated spiritual "smack down" (to borrow a phrase from the world of professional wrestling). The former persecutor of the church experienced the "shock and awe" of post-Easter mercy.

Philippians, as *all* of Paul's letters, includes a salutation that begins with the word *grace*. "Grace and peace to you from God our Father and the Lord Jesus Christ." We can be sure it was not a hollow shibboleth. "Amazing Grace" may have become a generic one-size-fits-all public domain anthem in our culture, but to Paul, grace was a fabulous, rejoice-in-the-Lord-always-and-again-I-say-rejoice life-changing surprise.

Paul held coats while people were stoned to death for being followers of the Way. After the surprise of grace he was willing to step in front of the stone throwers for the sake of the Way. The Way was the way of grace. So awesome is this gift that Paul will later affirm "at the name of Jesus every knee should bow, in heaven and on earth and under the earth, and every tongue confess that Jesus Christ is Lord, to the glory of God the Father" (2:10-11).

The incongruity of "cheap grace" was famously noted by German theologian and martyr Dietrich Bonhoeffer, in *The Cost of Discipleship*. Bonhoeffer's insistence that grace not be treated frivolously was exponentially reinforced by the ultimate cost of his own discipleship. Postmodern sensibilities may be offended at the affirmation of Hebrews 9:22, "without the shedding of blood there is no forgiveness," but grace is not cheap, especially to the Giver. The prophet Ezekiel hears these instructions from the Lord:

> Therefore groan, son of man! Groan before them with broken heart and bitter grief. And when they ask you, "Why are you groaning?" you shall say, "Because of the news that is coming. Every heart will melt and every hand go limp; every spirit will become faint and every knee will become as weak as water." It is coming! It will surely take place, declares the Sovereign LORD (21:6-7).

As "Amazing Grace" reminds us, "twas grace that taught my heart to fear." Grace leads us to groan as we face our rebellious hearts in light of God's love and truth. Then grace surprises us with mercy that only faith can humbly receive. "It is coming," God told Ezekiel. Paul knew it had come—the grace that melts every heart and makes every knee as weak as water and predestined to bow before the Lord.

Grace and peace to you from God the Father
and the Lord Jesus Christ.

There is no more vital discovery in life than to understand the grace of God. Grace can be defined in terms such as "undeserved favor" or "God's free gift of blessing." But grace most fully comes alive when we realize it has a face in the person of Jesus. Paul had written, "For no matter how many promises God has made, they are 'Yes' in Christ" (II Corinthians 1:20). Jesus said, "But I, when I am lifted up from the earth, I will draw all men to myself" (John 12:32). Both of these verses point to the living Christ as the primary source of grace in God's activity to rescue humankind from sin and death. For Paul to salute this congregation with grace and peace was to greet them in Christ.

A missionary attempted to translate the word *grace* as he worked on scripture translation. Working with a native of the area where he was laboring, he tried to communicate the meaning of grace in such a way as to enable his helper to offer an equivalent term. "It is a gift, a living gift," he said. Appearing to understand, the native assistant suggested a word from his language. In turn, the missionary used it in the verse that speaks of Jesus being "full of grace and truth." However, unbeknownst to him, he actually said Jesus was "full of chicken and truth."

In seminary my Hebrew professor Dr. John Oswalt loved to talk about a content-rich Hebrew word that parallels grace. The word is *hesed*. It means loving kindness. My favorite illustration of this takes place at the death of King Saul. David, King Saul's enemy, and Saul's son, Jonathan, are soul mates. It was traditional for a surviving leader, such as David, to kill any remaining members of an enemy's family that might live on as a threat. When David learned that Saul had another son who was still alive, Mephibosheth, he called for the surviving son to be brought to the throne room (2 Samuel 9). To Mephibosheth this must have sounded like the summons to his execution. On top of that, he was physically handicapped. Such an "unwhole" person, as they would have considered him in that day, normally had no personal dealings with a king.

As Mephibosheth entered the throne room he saw a banquet table spread, further evidence of his impending death. No "cripple" ate with a king. But to his amazement, David invited him to the table and offered his protection and provision.

I often think of this story when I come to "the King's table" for the Lord's Supper. As a spiritual "cripple," I am unworthy. As a sinner at heart I deserve no mercy. But God's living gift, his Son, extends *hesed*, grace to me. He invites me to the family meal and gives undeserved blessing out of the richness of his cross-scarred heart.

Grace is easier to describe than define. Robert De Moor recalls grace in action during the apple harvest days of his childhood. Five children were in his family. Each would be seated in front of a mountain of apples and given canning jars to fill.

His mother never bothered keeping track of who peeled how many apples. There was little doubt that the youngest ones were more of a problem than a help, with cut fingers and intermittent arguments over who used which pan and so on.

When the job was completed the reward was the same for everyone: the largest chocolate dipped cone money could buy. Was this fair? No. This was grace.

Discovering the Necessity of Grace

It is the undeserved kindness, the mercy, the grace of God that makes provision for whosoever will to come to Christ and be freed from condemnation and estrangement with him. A. W. Tozer, the great Canadian preacher who also pastored in the United States, has written, "No one was ever saved other than by grace . . . . Since mankind was banished from the eastward garden, none has ever returned to the divine favor except through the sheer goodness of God" (*The Knowledge of the Holy*, p. 102).

Paul is clear in all he writes. The great avenue of God's graciousness is Jesus Christ. The cross has become the bridge by which all may walk by faith into fellowship with God.

*Grace and peace to you from God the Father
and the Lord Jesus Christ*

In the Old Testament, contrary to what some may think, we find numerous expressions of grace. I have already alluded to David's experience with Mephibosheth. A more graphic example is the exodus of the Hebrews from Egyptian slavery. The Israelites were up against an impenetrable barrier which, in their own strength, they could not surmount. By the incredible grace of God, the sea parted and they were delivered. Even so, you and I are up against the impenetrable barrier of God's holiness, with our enemies—sin and death—at our heels. Only by the cross is our deliverance secured. That is grace, saving grace, one of many ways in which God expresses his kindness to us.

In the best-selling book *The Road Less Traveled*, psychiatrist Scott Peck includes a chapter entitled "The Miracle of Health." It is part of a larger section of the book that is labeled simply, "Grace." The essence of this chapter reflects Dr. Peck's astonishment that the push toward wholeness is surprisingly strong in human life.

As a therapist he notes his frequent amazement that people are not sicker than they are. He shares a story about a remarkably successful businessman who comes for counseling due to a mild neurosis. This man was born an illegitimate child. He was reared in a Chicago slum by his deaf and speechless mother. The state of Illinois, believing his mother to be incompetent, took him away at age five with no explanation or warning. A succession of three foster homes then followed, a period in which he experienced a total lack of affection. At fifteen he became partially paralyzed from the rupture of a congenital aneurysm in his brain. The following year he abandoned a final set of foster parents to live on his own. One year later he was jailed for a vicious assault. No psychiatric treatment was ever given.

Upon his release from jail he was offered a job as a stock clerk in a rather ordinary company. Within three years this young man had become the youngest department head in the history of the company. In five years, after marrying another executive, he left the company to form his own business, becoming relatively wealthy.

By the time he came to Dr. Peck for treatment, he had become a loving and effective father, a self-educated thinker, a community leader and an accomplished artist. How?

Scott Peck, who did not write *The Road Less Traveled* from a Christian-apologist stance, concluded there was but one answer, grace. Later in the chapter he asks, "Could it really be that the line in the song is true, "'Tis grace hath brought me safe thus far?'"

What holds the universe of relationships together?

Why, considering the evil and selfishness in the world, are things not worse?

Why does the human body tend to heal itself and be generally healthy in spite of millions of germs, abuse and disease?

Why do people sacrifice for others?

Why does anyone ever forgive?

The answer is the active graciousness of God in our world.

How does anyone ever decide to surrender to Christ, and how does anyone ever live a Christian life? Listen to Paul's answer from Ephesians 2:8-9, "For it is by grace you have been saved, through faith—and this is not from yourselves, it is a gift of God—not by works, so that no one can boast." Add to that I Corinthians 15:10, ". . . by the grace of God I am what I am, and his grace to me was not in vain. No, I worked harder than all of them—yet not I, but the grace of God that was in me."

The final benediction of the New Testament, Revelation 22:21, says, "The grace of the Lord Jesus be with God's people. Amen."

This is the greatest discovery a person can make—that God's grace is the foundation upon which everything is built. If you have spent your life trying to be good enough to please God, if you are waiting until you are good enough to claim to be a Christian, this is the best news ever announced. It is a gift; our salvation is a gift. Humbly embracing this fact and walking in amazed faith and gratitude is the heartbeat of a healthy believer and a Christian community.

*Grace and peace to you from God the Father
and the Lord Jesus Christ*

I recall with wonder and gratitude a naval officer who came to
see me in my early days as his pastor. He wanted me to know his
story. As he spoke, I could see his spiritual hands outstretched,
letting go of a "controlling" lifestyle. An adult child of an alcoholic,
he had ruined his life trying to control it. One of his children had
followed the example set by her father and mother in developing a
serious alcohol abuse problem. His marriage had disintegrated. In
the midst of his meltdown, he found his way (by grace) to church,
where the Holy Spirit used the pastor's words to touch his life and
bring him new insight and courage. Later, responding to an altar
call in a traditional revival service, he gave his controlling spirit
over to God.

In his newfound freedom he could admit that this did not solve all
of his problems. As many new Christians discover, God's grace can
bring a "sword" as well as peace. Taking a ruthless moral inventory
of his life, part of the Twelve Steps of Alcoholic's Anonymous, was
deeply painful. But like the surgeon's knife, the sword brought
healing. As is virtually always necessary, he found his way into a
support group, where in fear and trembling he could identify and
reject old thought patterns and habits. In that environment, he
found continuing grace available to help in living "on the stretch"
in faith.

As I listened to his story, I recognized it as a classic lose-your-
life-to-find-it narrative. We rejoiced together that the simple
prescription Jesus gave still works. Hands emptied of pride, fear,
anger and guilt—outstretched toward the Lord—are filled with
grace. I literally laughed as I often do when feeling deeply blessed
at the amazing nature of grace.

Not all the stories have happy endings. A woman who had come
for counseling prior to marriage seemed obviously in need of grace.
As we talked I told her that nothing she could do could make God

love her any more or any less. I added that we can always refuse that love or block grace by our sins and disobedience, but we can never earn it. At that point, about an hour into our conversation, she abruptly said, "Let's get on with why we're here." That was that. It became too uncomfortable for her when grace moved from a concept to a living gift with which she would have to reckon.

Grace Unfolds when We Exercise Faith

For grace to work in the life of the believer, it must extend beyond a doctrine. It must reach the heart, the nerves, the place where life decisions are made. Grace must be grace applied. In fact, there is a mathematics to faith—grace given + grace applied = peace. We must be able to say as Paul did, "His grace to me was not in vain."

E. Stanley Jones once said that "spiritual impression without spiritual expression leads to spiritual depression." In other words, believers must do more than experience God's grace. They must act upon it.

God's grace enters our lives to give us "response-ability." His Spirit enables us to say "yes" to him.

At the heart of our sinful nature is a deeply rooted desire to be in control of our lives. Invitation hymns such as "I Surrender All" call us to surrender control as a critical component to embracing grace. With fingernails dug into the pews as an altar call is given, we resist such a surrender, fearing a loss of control in our lives.

Oswald Chambers in his classic devotional guide *My Utmost for His Highest* (August 21), observes that the popular expression "decide for Jesus" is off the mark. We do not decide for him, we simply yield to him. But the result of that turns out to be just the opposite of what we fear. Instead of losing control, we discover that we actually have far greater control over ourselves than we previously had. Grace puts a bit in the mouths of our fleshly instincts.

The old myth continues to circulate that there are people who are absolutely free. Not so! Everyone serves someone. All freedom is relative to our circumstances. The person "free" to drink intemperately, use drugs, recklessly pursue wealth and success, achieve popularity, or pursue any other addiction, is a slave to that desire. The first lie ever told, that we could be like God, feeds this myth. Indeed, even God is not absolutely free. His love for us and his purity of will limits his choices and alternatives as far as we, with our finite limits, can understand such choices.

God's grace works in our lives to give us true freedom, the freedom to say "yes" to God's will. Within this freedom lies the closest thing to true self-control a person can know. But that power of choice must be exercised, that "response-ability" must be employed or grace is "in vain."

One of the oldest tensions in a grace-centered faith exists between so-called grace and law, or faith and works. I have already quoted from Ephesians 2 where Paul clearly notes that grace, not works, has saved him. If that is so, how do our works, our "responses," fit in? The answer to that depends on what we perceive the function of "works" to be.

Clearly, works of the law—specific moral actions in response to the commands of God—cannot be the source of our salvation. When works are a *quid pro quo*—a "this for that," an attempt to manipulate God—their motivation nullifies any link to salvation. Such works further reveal our need for grace. But works do not have to originate in our sin and insecurity. Their impulse can spring from grace already at work within us.

The function of good works, of obedience, is to act so as to give expression of our faith, trust and gratitude. The man who turns from pornography or the woman who refuses to gossip can find motivation in trusting that God is right in condemning such tempting behaviors. As Old Testament scholar and educator, Dennis Kinlaw has noted, all things are good if they are used as God directs. Good works are the godly use of all things, a stewardship of life based on faith rather than fear.

Grace and peace from God the Father and the Lord Jesus Christ.

Faith in Action is the Mechanism that Engages Faith

Expressing our faith through actions releases the power of God in our lives. This is not a reward for the action, but the God-ordained consequence of the action. The result is growth in grace and ultimate blessing from God. The area of life where this most commonly applies is in forgiving others. In the Lord's Prayer, Jesus notes that our own forgiveness is based on forgiving others, that is, applying it. Many of us try to win God's favor by helping the needy or teaching Sunday school or some such good deed. But forgiving those who have really hurt us seems to evade us. Forgiving is almost always an act of faith. Why is it we are so reluctant to forgive? Holding a grudge seems to give us a feeling of control (there's that word again) over others. In reality it is we who are being controlled, controlled by our anger and hate. It has been said that refusing to forgive someone is like drinking poison in the hope that the other person will die. In reality, the person in greatest control (with the most peace) is the one who appears to give up control over others and forgive.

Where does our failure to apply grace begin? It begins with our failure truly to receive grace. The story of the unforgiving servant is a case in point (Matthew 18: 21-35). David Seamands observed the amazing fact that the servant did not really receive the grace given by his lord. All he asked for, and all he accepted was an extension of time. "I will pay you back." Dr. Seamands also pointed out the ironic result of the servant's attempts to stay in control. He eventually ends up back in prison. Grace offered minus grace applied equals no peace.

It is obvious that God's grace, free though it is, calls for something we resist unless we are in charge of it—change. To accept grace as the foundation of our lives is to agree to make a fundamental change in our lives. It requires giving up an attitude of pride and independence before God, to repent and to surrender. It may sound easy enough to say, "I accept the gift of God's grace," but in reality it is an upheaval of one's perspective. I agree with Old Testament scholar Dennis Kinlaw when he observed, "True surrender is never a noble gesture; it is the capitulation of a rebel, no matter how much the unsanctified ego would like to make it otherwise." (*Preaching in the Spirit*, pp. 105-6). It is a humbling thing to receive and live by grace. The psychology of the altar call has this at its root. Both the public call and the altar of sacrifice reflect the dynamics of a profound acceptance of grace.

Such an acceptance of grace leads to a subtle but radical change of attitude in the heart.

Halford Luccock illuminated this change, writing,

> Self-denial, in a common use of the term, as abstaining from certain luxuries and delights, may even induce a sort of self-assertion, in applauding our own self-control and generosity, making spiritual Little Jack Horners out of ourselves, whispering, "What a good boy am I!" The denial of the *self* is something deeper. It is making ourselves not an end, but a means, in the kingdom of God" (*Interpreter's Bible* (7:770).

The application of grace leads to what Paul refers to as "having the mind of Christ." This mind is one that sees itself as a means and not an end, a change from normal human nature of the most basic sort. This is why it calls for a taking up of the cross. The cross symbolizes the call and power of grace to enable us to rise above our "end in ourselves" attitudes. I can picture a "Far Side"-style of cartoon depicting the scene at the cross. Everyone except Jesus is wearing a T-shirt that reads "End in Myself." What would your T-shirt read today?

Such root changes of spirit and attitude produce the fruit of altered behavior. There are relationships to be made right, if possible. There are emotional hang-ups to be faced. Priorities are to be reordered. Service is to be performed. Giving is to be done. We have to reckon with a new kind of self-love and self-acceptance.

Professor and author Dallas Willard calls for "bodily behaviors of faith" to be learned—the disciplines of prayer, study, worship, fasting and meditation. This is the process of our sanctification, the working out of our salvation in fear and trembling. It is the work of a lifetime. I affirm the realism of David Seamand's pastoral conclusion, "The truth is that God Himself is going to slow down our pace, for He has no shortcuts to spiritual growth and maturity" (*Healing of Memories*, p. 181).

The question of each new day is: Do I love the Lord today? Am I, because of gratitude for his grace, willing to take the next step to which God is calling me? Do we desire more grace? Scott Peck says that one of the norms of psychiatric practice is that the great majority of patients stop therapy rather than deal with the changes that their healing would require. He goes on to say,

> To be aware of grace, to personally experience its constant presence, to know one's nearness to God, is to know and continually experience an inner tranquility and peace that few possess. On the other hand, this knowledge brings with it an enormous responsibility . . . . The call to grace is a call to a life of effortful caring, to a life of service and whatever sacrifice seems required. It is a call out of spiritual childhood into adulthood, a call to be a parent unto mankind. (pp. 301-2)

This is where "becoming like a child" will lead—true maturity.

God so loved the world that He gave His only begotten Son

In that moment of infinite grace the call begins in earnest, the call to kneel at the cross while we are yet sinners, humble ourselves, and with spiritual hands outstretched seek a rebirth of spirit. As "all things become new" (2 Corinthians 5:17), we can begin to do the mathematics of faith. No shortcuts can be found to peace or maturity. Grace is free. The daily call comes to apply that grace in faithful obedience, and it brings with it the life-altering peace of God that follows. A living faith and a true Christian community live and breathe by grace through faith. Amazing!

Questions for Discussion

1. Have you ever hit bottom in any respect in your relationship with God? If so, how did you get to that point? What did it teach you about grace?

2. Why is grace not "fair"? What is the difference between God being just and being fair?

3. Where in your life has God's grace "brought you safe" when you were unaware of it at the time?

4. If Jesus took a ruthless moral inventory of your life, what would it reveal?

5. Has God's grace ever seemed threatening to you?

6. Who and what do you feel you must control? How important is control to you?

7. What does it mean to say that our greatest freedom comes from saying "Yes" to God's will? Why do we fear God's will?

8. What do you think of Bonhoeffer's declaration "only those who obey believe"?

9. What does your freedom (or lack thereof) to forgive others tell you about your understanding of God's forgiveness of you? Why?

10. What is the difference in seeing ourselves as means rather than ends in God's kingdom?

CHAPTER THREE

Remaining in His Outstretched Hands

(God Is at Work for Good)

Philippians 1:6
. . . being confident of this, that he who began a good work in you will carry it on to completion until the day of Christ Jesus

"Give me a place to stand and I will move the earth."

Archimedes' confident claim in the face of an apparent impossibility echoes a longing in every human heart. We dream of a place, an intellectual, emotional, volitional and spiritual place where the weight of our inconsistent selves can be lifted to a higher, consistent plane. But knowing ourselves, we live in doubt, if not cynicism. Sigmund Freud offers no comfort in his evaluation of human potential, saying, "I have found little that is good about human beings on the whole. In my experience most of them are trash no matter whether they publicly subscribe to this or that ethical doctrine or to none at all" (quoted in *Cries of the Heart*, R. Zacharias, p. 126). Even so, we continue to dream and hope.

Pulitzer Prize winning author Robert Coles, designated by a *Time* magazine cover story in 1972 as "the most influential living psychiatrist in the U.S.," describes human experience in these words, "We walk a tightrope, teetering between gloom, or the loss of faith, on the one hand, and a temptation toward self-importance and self-congratulation on the other" (quoted in *Soul Survivor*, P. Yancey, p. 116). We are an admixture of pride and shame, hope and fear, walking a tightrope while looking for a place to stand.

We Look for a Way to Live with Our Imperfect Discipleship

Satan, who should take a vacation but never seems to, is far more consistent than we are. Every day he earns his nickname, "the accuser": "How can you call yourself a Christian? You know what you did! You know what you thought! You know the things you didn't do that you should have done!" Depending on how sensitive we are, such accusations can become amplified in our minds to a deafening level. The "still small voice" of God's Spirit (1 Kings 19:12, *KJV*) is drowned out by the persistence of recurring negative suggestions, dripping into our soul like Chinese water torture. Christians will usually respond to this according to their theology.

Those of the once-saved-always-saved stripe may respond to self-doubt by digging in to the point of cheap grace: "God forgives me no matter what." John Wesley, father of Methodism, experienced his greatest opposition because he resisted such an attitude. At the same time he said, "I am a hair's breadth from Calvinism." (Calvinism generally holds a strong view that salvation is based on God's sovereign choice alone and once given cannot be lost.) Wesley was very comfortable with acknowledging that "the wind blows where it wills" (John 3:8), and God will dispense grace as he chooses. Yet Wesley maintained that hair's breadth of human "response-ability," believing "antinomianism" to be an attitude of moral carelessness. The Christian faith must be, he maintained, more than a spiritual perfume that covers the stench but does not transform the individual.

The free-will folks, on the other hand, take their spiritual pulse and usually find it uncertain or inconclusive. These people (and I have related to many of them) if asked, "Are you saved?" will sincerely reply, "I hope so." Such a hope usually reflects more self-doubt than humility.

Elsewhere on the continuum of faith, self-doubt may express itself through an obsession with certain "supernatural" phenomena, dramatic spiritual gifts most often, as the clear evidence of salvation. Others fasten onto involvement with human hurts as the anesthesia for this ache of uncertainty. Apart from a clear foundation of salvation by grace through faith, all of these responses are manifestations of pride, a deep-seated desire to be in control.

> *being confident of this, that he who began a good work in you will carry it on to completion until the day of Christ Jesus.*

Psychoanalyst Karen Horney, who pioneered such terms as alienation and self-realization, in her book *Neurosis and Human Growth*, delves deeply into the inner dynamics of human personality as we attempt to cope with unconscious drives. While sharing insights that reflect the incredible complexity of our psyches, she concludes that deep dissatisfaction with our selves (she speaks of self-hate) arises from subconscious desires for god-like perfection. "According to my views, the inner dictates are an expression of the individual's unconscious drive to make himself over into something he is not (a god-like, perfect being), and he hates himself for not being able to do so" (p. 374). In a nutshell this is paradise lost, the human alternation between poverty of spirit and narcissism, between faithfulness and self-absorption.

C. S. Lewis, former atheist and late well-known Christian apologist, was acquainted with the roller coaster ride that Christians experience in struggling with themselves. He viewed it as a manifestation of what he termed "the law of undulation." This "law" is a corollary to the fact that human beings are finite and physical as well as sinful. Our lives more closely resemble an up-and-down radio wave than a straight line. Regardless of the overall quality of our discipleship, the inner uncertainty represented by this "law" seems to give the lie to any hope that we are living a truly faithful life.

Walking by faith in Jesus Christ means a determination to locate the place where we stand, i.e., the location of our identity as believers, beyond our efforts in and of ourselves. At the same time we remember that if our new identification with Jesus Christ is real, the content of our behavior will change as well. Wesley, in his "hair's-breadth" position, was affirming that 99% of what takes place in the Christian faith is based on what God in Christ has done, is doing and will do (change our status before God). He refused to relinquish the other 1% because our faith (our God-assisted capacity to react to grace and thus experience a change in self) is located in that small portion of the total.

As a young Christian coming from the "free-will" stance, I recall hearing a pastor say, "Imagine that you were in business and you went to someone soliciting his involvement in your enterprise. He might look at you and indicate that he is sorry, but you did not inspire enough confidence for him to take a chance on doing business with you. Now imagine that you approach the same person. This time you make your pitch, and then you add that your partner in this endeavor is Bill Gates (of Microsoft). How do you think the reaction would be different?" The answer is obvious. As Christians we are in "partnership" with the Lord of the universe. His "credit line" of grace and truth is infinite. As his partners we must give 100% just as he does. But we must never forget the source of our spiritual "capital." Neither should we forget that while his investment is what makes our faith possible, we forfeit our partnership benefits if we withhold our own small but essential contributions.

Yes, the analogy is simplistic. But it is fundamentally valid. It points to the fact that we are not alone in our Christian journey. Indeed, we have a Companion who is not on the same roller coaster ride we often find ourselves experiencing. He is the objective fact of our Christian life that can carry us through. He is the Alpha, the One whose grace begins our Christian journey, and by our faith in his faithfulness. He is also the Omega, the One who takes us safely to the end. He guarantees the security of our "investment," at the same time calling us to affirm our partnership and our faith by making our humble investment of ourselves each day.

Paul Proclaims a Place to Stand

So where is our confidence? Listen as we read Philippians 1:6 from *The Living Bible*, ". . . I am sure that God who began the good work within you will keep right on helping you grow in His grace until His task within you is finally finished on that day when Jesus Christ returns." This is the source of our confidence—God, the same yesterday, today, and forever, does not change, is not on a roller coaster. God will continue to work within us until the end. Why do we dare call ourselves Christian? How do we dare believe we can grow in grace? Because of our commitment? Because of our family heritage? Because of our gifts and talents? Because we are hard workers? Because of our good intentions? No. None of these are adequate foundations. "On Christ the solid rock we stand, all other ground is sinking sand." His are the "deep pockets" of grace that secure the often shaky commitment of ourselves we make by faith. This must be clear if we are to stand firm throughout the years of our faith journey.

Biblical faith begins with the understanding that every human life is born in debt to the living God who created everything. God began a good work in us all on the day he first commanded, "Let there be light." From the onset of the Creation, God has been providing the priceless gifts of that creation, a dependable universe abundant in resources. In this God we have confidence, and it is his world in which we are guests.

Some years ago a New York law firm was engaged to clear a deed in Louisiana. The lawyer in Louisiana said he could trace the title back to 1803 when the United States purchased the territory from France. However, the big city law firm was not satisfied. They insisted on information further back. The southern lawyer, fed up with their demands, finally wrote back:

Sirs,
Please be advised that France acquired title from Spain by conquest. The Spanish obtained it through discovery by

Christopher Columbus, a sailor who had been authorized by Isabella, Queen of Spain, who obtained sanction from the Pope, who is vicar of Christ, who is the heir of God Almighty, who made Louisiana!

God in his creation has begun a good work.

In college I wrote a short story about hell. While short stories tend to be by nature fiction, this one was definitely the fruit of my imagination. The picture of hell that came to me can be wrapped up in one word—unpredictability. Everything from gravity to the musical scale worked fine one minute and then did not work at all. Imagining such a life served to awaken in me a real appreciation of this world as we know it. While unpredictable things do happen, they are far and away the exception.

In an ironic way, the results of sin in this normally dependable universe have the effect of bringing hell into our lives. The child who never knows whether he will be hugged or slugged by a dysfunctional parent certainly experiences the atmosphere of hell. The spouse whose partner is unfaithful is braised with the fires of hell. No one appreciates the predictable gravity of truthfulness like the victim of a lie. Sin is the crooked line that throws into relief the straightedge of God's truth. That truth is seen, not only in his Word, but also in his world.

The Unseen God is Always at Work

being confident of this, that he who began a good work in you will carry it on to completion until the day of Christ Jesus

God in his creation has begun a good work. But he has done more than give us a wondrous world in which to live. He has given us himself, taking the initiative to bring us back to him. "You see, at just the right time, when we were still powerless, Christ died for the ungodly. . . . God demonstrates his own love for us in this:

While we were still sinners, Christ died for us" (Romans 5: 6, 8). That is, before we sought him, he sought us. "The Son of Man came to seek and to save the lost" (Luke 19:10). "For this is what the Sovereign Lord says: I myself will search for my sheep and look after them" (Ezekiel 34:11).

Some Christians refer to this as "prevenient grace." An old-fashioned term from the post-King James era used in the same way as "preventing" grace, it was often on John Wesley's tongue. We can understand its meaning in that day if we consider the word vent. When something is vented, a way is opened for it. "God, Who has opened a way for us, will continue to open a way for us until the day of Christ Jesus." John indicates that this starts at the beginning of our lives, "The true light that gives light to every man was coming into the world" (John 1:9).

Light and grace are given to every person. An ancient heathen legend tells of a day when human beings stood before the gods, daring to be godlike. These god "wannabes" knew that the gods had a unique quality about them, a god-spark. It was this spark that the humans coveted. Possessing such a light, they could stride across the earth with unbridled pride. However, the gods wanted no rivals. The legend goes on to say that the gods held tightly to the spark. Every effort was made to prevent humans from possessing it, though they continued to be naturally inquisitive. They traversed the continents, swam the oceans, and searched the skies, unwilling to leave any stone unturned in their relentless search for the god-spark. At last, one day the great god Brahm stood up before the gods and signaled for silence. There was a self-satisfied smile of victory on his face. "Fear not," he told his fellow gods, "for I have found the place to hide the spark forever. It is a spot which they shall never think to search. I have hidden it deep in their hearts" (J. W. Hamilton, *Still the Trumpet Sounds*, pp. 116-17).

This old tale reflects a universal awareness that the heart was made for greater things. The image of God found in every life calls for some kind of explanation. That "eternity in the heart" of which

Ecclesiastes speaks (3:11), the "light that lights every person," brings with it a potential for which even writers of myth had to find an explanation. The explanation is not hard to find. It is the grace of God, both the common grace that glues the world together and the prevenient grace of God that "vents" in such a way that people can get in touch with their Creator and Redeemer.

Of course, the foundation of this possibility was not some sort of naturally available spark. The foundation for human beings to fulfill their potential, as Paul saw it, was the action of God in Jesus Christ. Jesus himself had said, "If I be lifted up I will draw all men unto myself" (John 12:32). Christ had been lifted up on the cross and then raised up on Easter. In the mystery of redemption, these events gave freedom to the Father to pour out his Spirit. Quakers call it the "double search," the human search for God paralleled by the divine search for people, and it began in a new and living way. It continues, by grace, to this day.

When the apostle Paul stood before King Agrippa, he proclaimed that his call from Jesus on the Damascus Road pointed to God's search for his children. "I am sending you to them to open their eyes and turn them from darkness to light, and from the power of Satan to God, so that they may receive forgiveness of sins and a place among those who are sanctified by faith in me" (Acts 26:17-18).

As I began my first year of college, my brother, Jerry, was in Vietnam, flying helicopters. Jerry and I were different. He was always dating, always partying. I was more studious and serious. But Jerry had a huge heart. There have been times when I have thought that he, not I, should have been the pastor. But it was not to be. During the so-called Tet offensive, when hundreds of young men lost their lives, Jerry became another casualty of war.

During spring break, several weeks after his death, I was home from college when his effects were delivered. It was a very moving experience to sort through them, looking for signs of what his last days were like. Among his things was a large calendar. The squares for each day were generously sized and Jerry had used them to keep something of a diary. On the Sunday before he was killed we read these words: "Today I took Communion." I cannot exaggerate the sense of wonder and gratitude that those words birthed in my heart. I was grateful for the chaplain, whoever he was, who risked his life in the field for people like my brother. And more, I was profoundly grateful to God whose grace could not be held back by the gates of hell in that place. Was it a "godforsaken" place? There is no such place. The God in whose name Jerry was baptized was determined to continue to seek his child, opening the way for a relationship regardless of the circumstances. God is always at work for good.

Pastor Roy Putnam wrote that mosquito wings beat 35,220 times per minute, the perfect rate of vibration needed to create the ideal tone for the growing of corn. The presence of this "tone," he says, has the capacity to stimulate corn so it will grow twice as fast as it otherwise would. Apparently, some scientists believe that each plant is responsive to an insect wing beat. As a Southerner for many years now, I would wonder if pine trees or cotton respond to the wing beats of gnats! Bananas are now grown on plantations with a certain tune played constantly to stimulate their growth (Roy Putnam, *Getting It All Together*, p. 22).

Such unseen stimulation escapes our normal senses. So it often is with the unseen work of God. Your reading of this book is not a random act, unrelated to any other action. It is part of God's venting in your life, to help you draw nearer to him. The Philippians had experienced this prior-venting (to go before) in their lives. God through Christ was at work to bring them to completion. Paul's letter was written to encourage them to respond to his outstretched hands in a similar posture of faith and gratitude.

When my wife was teaching French at Mercer County High School near Harrodsburg, Kentucky, during my seminary years, she helped organize an annual "French Day." A great deal of planning went into the event, and there were activities all through the day. As the school day began, one of the members of the French Club announced over the intercom that the club had placed a *fleur-de-lis* somewhere in the school building. Anyone who found it could claim a prize in Mrs. Adams' room. The hitch was that none of these kids had any idea what a *fleur-de-lis* looked like. While it was put in a prominent spot where it could be seen all day, various students brought in what they thought were *fleur-de-lis*, but none actually identified it correctly.

Our inability to recognize God at work in no way alters the reality of pre-venting grace (the grace that goes before). Only eternity will reveal just how often God nudged, pulled, pushed and inspired us to exercise our "response-ability." Archbishop William Temple of the Church of England was known to say, "I find that when I pray, coincidences happen."

At the end of his highly acclaimed series of interviews with Bill Moyers on Public Television, Joseph Campbell, authority on mythology and religions, used an interesting expression. He referred to persons for whom faith is not a part of their lives as being "without any invisible means of support." It is God's invisible means of support that works to carry us through to a complete relationship with himself for all eternity.

Don't Omit the Most Important Fact

being confident of this, that he who began a good work in you will carry it on to completion until the day of Christ Jesus.

A family in a church I was serving was confronted with a sudden and unexplainable illness in their very young daughter. Waiting with them one day, a bubbly nurse came into the hospital room, where the atmosphere was noticeably heavy with concern. This ray of sunshine mentioned that a co-worker, annoyed by her bubbly spirit, had asked her what an optimist is. His answer—someone who doesn't have all the facts. Persons of faith, like Archbishop Temple and Joseph Campbell, might reply that the opposite is true. It is the pessimist who lacks all the relevant facts. The facts are not exhausted by what the eye can see. God is at work.

Think back on your own life. What coincidences have happened that lead to good things? A high school principal, with whom my wife worked, was in the hospital apparently dying of an undiagnosable illness. By "coincidence" his doctor just happened to open a medical journal on a stack of books on his desk. The journal just happened to contain an article describing not only the exact symptoms of this unknown problem, but also the treatment. Why such "Godincidences" do not always happen, I do not know. But that does not change the fact that all along they do happen.

Perhaps God brings coincidences into our lives more often than we know. The gentleness with which they come may fail to grab our attention. A story I ran across a few years ago spoke volumes to me about the way in which God's intervention might take place, and yet how it is so often missed.

A mother and dad were endeavoring to teach their young son responsibility. Part of his training included telephoning home when he arrived at a friend's house a few blocks away. As boys will do, he began to grow negligent about the calls, growing more confident in himself to make the trip without any problems. The first time he forgot, his dad called to make sure he had arrived. If it happened again, they explained, he would have to turn around and come home. A few days later, he headed off to his friend's house, and again the telephone remained silent. What were his parents to do? They felt he should be punished to teach him a lesson, but they were reluctant to punish him. His father went to the telephone, regretting that his son's fun time would be interrupted by a disciplining parent. As the father dialed, he prayed for wisdom. "Treat him as I treat you," the Lord seemed to say. On the first ring of the telephone, the father hung up. A few seconds later the phone rang, and it was his son.

"I'm here, Dad!"

"What took you so long to call?" his dad asked.

"We started playing and I forgot. But Dad, I heard the phone ring once and I remembered."

"I'm glad you remembered," his dad replied. "Have fun" (*Leadership*, Sept. 1985, Vol. VI, #2, p. 69).

We must not expect God's at-work-before-we-know-it grace to look like the Red Sea parting every time it goes into action. More often than not it will take the form of the above story, anonymous and wise. If you have glimpsed God at work in this manner, you have likely felt the kind of dynamics expressed in these lines:

> I asked God for strength that I might achieve.
> I was made weak that I might learn humbly to obey.
> I asked God for health that I might do greater things.
> I was given infirmity that I might do better things.
> I asked for riches that I might be happy.
> I was given poverty that I might be wise.
> I asked for power that I might have the praise of men.
> I was given weakness that I might feel the need of God.
> I asked for all things that I might enjoy life.
> I was given life that I might enjoy all things.
> I got nothing that I asked for—
> but everything I had hoped for.
> Almost despite myself, my unspoken prayers were answered.
> I among all people am most richly blessed (quoted in Swindoll, *Excellence*, p. 113).

In the mystery of God's leading, I spent my college years in an evangelical Christian environment. Altar calls, like those given by Billy Graham at the end of his messages, were frequent. Most of the time, however, the invitation was not a call to salvation but to a holy life. Whatever the intention of those preachers, I now realize what I was looking for when I went forward to pray as the closing hymn was sung. I was looking for a Christian experience that would effectively make me autonomously free from temptation and sin. What a deal that would be! Why, I would live above the struggle of life and practically be like God! What I really wanted was to be free of my need for God. By his grace and truth, I am moving beyond that subtle search for control to the glorious liberty of the children of God.

It sounds similar to the early chapters of Genesis. I do not pretend to understand why God does not just zap us with overwhelming grace and end our struggle. Having said that, I fully understand it is in the struggle that we exercise the thing that pleases God the most: faith. It is clear that even God's Son, who modeled perfection for humankind, never attempted to live a faithful, obedient life apart from abiding in his Father. That was his place to stand.

Everyone is looking for a place to stand. For those of us who believe in Jesus Christ, that place is not in ourselves. While we must, in faith, reach out our hands, it is the mighty grasp of our Lord who holds us steady. Abiding in those hands each day, we can stand in confidence that he who has begun a good work in us will never quit working. One day he will bring it all to completion. Until then we lean hard on the great Protector of our souls and find a place to stand as we are held together by his grace.

Questions for Discussion

1. Can you relate to the tightrope Robert Coles describes as, walking between the poles of pride and shame, ego and inferiority? How does it influence your life?

2. How do you cope with self-accusation? When is it positive? When is it negative?

3. How would you respond to the question, "Are you saved?"

4. What does it mean to you that God in Christ can guarantee the security of your investment of yourself in God?

5. When Jesus spoke of "the widow and the orphan" he was speaking of the category of persons who are unable to provide for themselves. How does this classification of need affect how Christian compassion is directed?

6. Where has God's prevenient grace been at work in your life?

7. Jesus spoke of believers receiving "forgiveness of sins and a place among those who are sanctified by faith in me." What do think Jesus had in mind when he spoke of being sanctified by faith?

8. What difference does it make to believe that God in Christ took (and takes) the initiative to redeem our souls?

9. Someone observed that God is sometimes like a person playing hide-n-seek who clears his throat to give a hint that he is there. Have you ever felt this way?

10. Why are we not made fully mature when we first yield to Jesus?

Remaining in His Affection
(Seeking to Share God's Singlemindedness)

Philippians 1:7-11
It is right for me to feel this way about all of you, since I have you in my heart; for
whether I am in chains or defending and confirming the gospel,
all of you share in God's grace with me. God can testify how I long for all of you
with the affection of Christ Jesus.
And this is my prayer: that your love may abound more and more in knowledge
and depth of insight, so that you may be able to discern what is best and may be
pure and blameless until the day of Christ, filled with the fruit of righteousness that
comes through Jesus Christ—to the glory and praise of God.

Cartoonist Tim Liston exposed the truth about what often passes for our burdens concerning others when he depicted a man in the following situation:

> Oh, great! Here comes Bob: I told him I'd pray for him!
> Dear God, help Bob. Amen.
> Hey, Bob, been prayin' for you! (*Leadership*, Fall 1996,
> Vol. XVII, No. 4, p. 101)

Fortunately, some people carry their prayer burden more seriously than Bob's friend.

Praying with the Love of Jesus

In Philippians 1: 7-11, it becomes increasingly obvious that Paul's words are not like that "prayer" for Bob. In verse eight Paul says he longs for the people in this congregation with "the affection of

Christ Jesus." The Greek term for "affection" is *splangkna*. We find the same root word used by Jesus in Matthew 9:36 when he looked out on a crowd of lost people and felt compassion for them; they appeared to him like sheep without a shepherd. Paul was stirred by Christ-like compassion and it brought him to his knees. Like a parent who deeply desires maturity in his children, Paul wants the Philippian believers to be thoroughly transformed by the indwelling influence of Christ.

This strong connection with the needs of others reminds me of a popular drawing of Jesus. Its simple image mirrors the *splangkna* of the Lord. In this depiction the Good Shepherd is holding a lamb, nuzzling it close to his face, which is partially hidden by the lamb. Jesus' left hand is pulling the lamb tightly to himself. On the back of Jesus' hand is a small scar, a subtle reminder of *splangkna's* price. The Lord's eyes are closed as he concentrates on the needs of the lamb. The result of connecting with Jesus' compassion is written on the lamb's face: utter peace, security and rest. You can almost hear it sigh with relief.

What could be more renewing than to receive Christ's *splangkna*?

Such is the deep love Jesus expressed in Luke 13: 34, when he cried out, "O Jerusalem, Jerusalem, you who kill the prophets and stone those sent to you, how often I have longed to gather your children together, as a hen gathers her chicks under her wings, but you were not willing!" We seldom come closer to observing the pathos felt in the compassionate heart of God than in this spontaneous revelation of longing. Through Jesus we begin to understand that God's *splangkna* is not satisfied with bandages, with the therapeutic hug of the aforementioned drawing. The heart of God wants us to be children of God, like Christ in our maturity and fruitfulness. This is a burden the depth of which can be exposed only by the cross.

Listen as the affection, the burden, the longing of Jesus prays through Paul.

> And this is my prayer: that your love may abound more
> and more in knowledge and depth of insight, so that you
> may be able to discern what is best and may be pure and
> blameless until the day of Christ, filled with the fruit of
> righteousness that comes through Jesus Christ—to the glory
> and praise of God.

While I find these words thrilling in the potential they suggest for
our lives in Christ, I also find the compassion-driven words of Jesus
to Jerusalem most haunting, "How often I have longed to gather
your children together . . . but you were not willing" (Luke 13:34).

In spite of the deep affection of Jesus and the awesome possibilities
it opens up, our human hearts are quite at home in this fallen
world, where we are supposed to be aliens. We feel that all is well
when in reality the wages of an unbelieving, disobedient, fearful
life is killing our souls. In my role as a supervisor of churches, I
see congregations that have "saved their lives" from the cost of
discipleship while living in denial that it was destroying them. Why
is it that fifty percent of the congregations in the United States are
home to only about 10 percent of the country's church members?
Beyond demographics, a sobering part of the answer is found in
"Christian unwillingness" to submit to the transforming, costly
yet healing, compassionate, perfect love of Jesus. They could have
been loved to life by allowing the affection of Jesus to help them
overcome their fears and open their doors to new people, different
races, Christ-centered purposes. Elder brothers of the prodigal,
whose stubborn natures sometimes dominate congregations, have
little idea what their unwillingness costs them. Contented converts
fear overzealousness more than missing out on abundant life. And
God's pathos continues.

*And this is my prayer: that your love may abound more and more in
knowledge and depth of insight so that you may be able to discern
what is best.*

Paul wanted every person who would encounter this letter to know they were included in Jesus' love, his perfect, sanctifying love. The expression "you all" is used nine times as he makes a conscious effort to be sure each person takes his words to heart. So, I believe we who read the prayer Paul prays out of the affection of Jesus are now free to claim it for ourselves. This perfect love has power to cast out fear, overcome the flesh and make room for knowledge and insight, discernment and purity, healthful righteousness and the glorification of God.

For most of us this means a continuous openness to life at a new spiritual address, the Kingdom of God.

A Prayer for New Citizenship

If you find yourself in a culture other than your own, you have a choice to make: Am I going to live here as a visitor or a tourist, or do I want to become a citizen? This prayer is Paul's way of calling upon God to help super-naturalize the Philippian believers into citizenship in the kingdom of God.

I did not always live in the South. My roots are in the Midwest. But I knew when I loaded my worldly possessions on that moving van years ago it was not for a visit. I was going to become a citizen of my new surroundings. For the past twenty-plus years I have participated in a long-term course entitled "South Georgia Culture." It has been a most enjoyable class, and is part of the core curriculum for transplants who desire to live in the South. Eating grits, having long casual conversations, learning to love pine straw and a myriad of other cultural characteristics have gradually become a part of my life. I sometimes speak of myself as a "recovering Yankee," but I am not a visitor. I am a citizen.

Becoming a Christian is like moving to a new country, a new culture. "All things become new" in their potential as 2 Corinthians 5:17 tells us. But such a new start is only the beginning of dealing with the deepest part of ourselves. We move beyond justification to sanctification, which is the experience of moving from a change in status (pardoned) to a change in self (child of God); from a change of relationship to a change of heart. It calls for a depth of insight into both our potential and the obstacles within us that prevent us from fulfilling that potential. Paul prays for this sort of insight because he is interested in making disciples, not just converts. No one becomes a disciple by accident.

Anyone who has lived in another country understands the cultural differences one must deal with in a new setting. Stanley Key served as a missionary in France for a decade, learning a great deal about cross-cultural experiences. He attempted to instruct some French friends to play softball, but translating such terms as foul ball, home plate, you're out, ball, tag up and short stop proved challenging. Learning began with the facts and the terminology, but something within was needed to motivate them to work through a period of ignorance and misunderstanding. For example, it took awhile for them to accept a strike called against them when they had not even swung at the ball. It was tantamount to entering a new world.

Dr. Scott Peck, in *The Road Less Traveled and Beyond*, made this observation relevant to our pre-sanctification life. Whenever someone asks the question, "What is human nature?" his first answer is "Human nature is to go to the bathroom in your pants" (p. 212). It is human nature to do what we want to do when we want to do it. We want our needs met. Period. We are living under the domination of affection, affection for ourselves.

The common experience of socialization during childhood is the process of learning how to put a bit in the mouth of our needs and self-focus so as to guide them in acceptable, beneficial ways. Most converts to the Christian faith do not initially grasp the significance of the call to Christian socialization, or repentance. We simply do not have the insight needed to grasp or overcome our self-centered defensiveness. So there is always a need for the kind of prayer Paul is praying. Only in the context of love can we lower our defenses to the extent that knowledge and insight can be revealed and received. Practically speaking, this is why small groups have become so central to ministry. Most people need long-term loving relationships to enable them to experience the *splangkna* of Jesus.

And this is my prayer: that your love may abound more and more in knowledge and depth of insight.

Our needs bring us to Jesus—our needs for forgiveness, community, and meaning. But this is only the beginning. Somewhere along the journey we must go deeper, experiencing the inner sight that reveals our rebellious selves. Writing about this need in adolescents, pastor and author Eugene Peterson observes,

> I don't think . . . that simply because adolescents sometimes speak in moral tones they suddenly acquire moral authority. Their insights do not suddenly catapult them into a position of superiority. Finding stupidity, intransigence, and evil where they did not expect it . . . is only the beginning of their moral education. Someday they will find it in themselves; and when they do they will no longer be kids . . . . (quoted in "Youth Ministry in Adolescence: Mistaking Cynicism For Discernment," Duffy Robbins, *Good News*, Jan./Feb., 2005, p. 29).

Our needs, including the granddaddy of them all, control, must be recognized and surrendered (again and again) to the forgiving, transforming touch of grace.

But getting back to Dr. Peck, when asked the same question about human nature, he also facetiously responds "there is no such thing" (p. 213). He continues,

> For what distinguishes us humans from most other creatures is not our opposable thumb or our magnificent larynx or our huge cerebral cortex; it is our relative lack of instincts, those inherited, preformed patterns of behavior

that, as far as we can ascertain, give the other creatures a much more fixed and predetermined nature than we have as humans. In other words, human beings are endowed with access to a much wider range of options—socially, psychologically, and physically—that give us flexibility in responding and handling a variety of circumstances and situations.

Such a cornucopia of choice opens the door to both creative disobedience and "more and more knowledge and depth of insight" as creatures made in God's image. While we are not bound by the narrow instincts found in the animal world, we are born with a basic instinct to place ourselves at the center of the universe.

The new birth in Christ renews our relationship with God. It does not remove our capacity for self-love. To do so would be contrary to our original design. Rather, it opens the door for the transformation of our needs, of our knowledge and depth of insight regarding those needs so that self-love can find its compass in Christ. David Seamands offers an illustration on how long-standing Christians can still grow in knowledge, insight and love.

He was preaching on the Great Commandment to love God with all your heart, as well as to love your neighbor as yourself. Later a man approached him and said, "As old as I am, I have never before actually heard Jesus' words correctly.

"While you were preaching, I suddenly realized that with my lips I have said, 'Love thy neighbor as thyself,' but deep down in my inner self I have really been hearing, 'Love thy neighbor but hate thyself.' I'm afraid I have been scrupulously living up to that commandment as I translated it" (*Healing for Damaged Emotions*, p. 71).

Such insight was the sort of answer Paul would hope for from this prayer.

A Prayer to Grow in Love Like God's

filled with the fruit of righteousness that comes through Christ Jesus.

To the extent that prayers for insight have been answered in my own life, I have seen that the bottom line of all that is prayed for in Philippians 1:9-11—knowledge, depth of insight, discernment, purity, blamelessness and righteousness—is found in God's love. Paul's prayer is essentially a prayer to grow in the love of God.

Christian purity, blamelessness and righteousness is a manifestation of love. Danish theologian Søren Kirkegaard wrote a book entitled *Purity of Heart Is to Will One Thing.* The title itself reflects a fact about God. God's purity is more than moral purity, i.e., sinlessness. God's purity is an awesome single-mindedness. God has but one purpose: to love. To ask God for purity, blamelessness and righteousness is to make a request to share in his single-mindedness.

The word "purity" suggests something being tested by sunlight. For our purposes, it is the sunlight of God's love. If the window shades of our motives were suddenly raised, what would the light of God's love reveal? Would we be blameless? Righteous?

God's "Son-light" of love contains the dynamics to overpower the shadows of rationalization by which we normally protect ourselves from blame. One of the most brilliant sources of Christian light for many Christian lives has been the pen of Oswald Chambers. Concerning the topic of obedience, Chambers reiterated this point. He thought that as soon as we find ourselves bogged down in questions over God's will, we can be fairly sure we are avoiding obedience in some way. At such times the inclination to "will one thing," namely our own will, turns us into spinmeisters, blame handlers. Rationalization overshadows truth when we attempt to appease our conscience. Rather than asking, "What would be the loving thing to do?" we instinctively consider the less painful or more pleasant thing, and we justify our course of action.

Giving is a classic case in point. "It would be easy to give ten percent if we made only $100 a week. But at our family's income, who can afford it?"

To that line of reasoning, logic would ask, "When do you have the most left over for yourself? When you have 90 percent of $100 or 90 per cent of $500 or $1,000, etc.?" Someone once said that tithing is God's way of letting people with money off the hook. Reason agrees with that, doesn't it? Purity and singleness of purpose go much deeper than morality. Paul would have said that singleness of mind goes deeper than the "law."

Michael Slaughter, pastor of the dynamic Ginghamsburg United Methodist Church near Dayton, Ohio, writes of a season in that congregation's life when obedience opened the door to transformation. The church had planned an "adopt a family" program for the Christmas Season of 1979. In previous years such efforts had resulted in cheap gifts from the local discount store, or less than that, giving away of hand-me-downs. But this year something different happened. Church members began to sense that the Holy Spirit was prodding them to do more, much more. Across the congregation people decided to spend as much on adopted families as they spent on themselves. Christmas Eve that year was so joyful as they worshiped and sang the carols of the season.

And what did God say about all this?

"You hypocrites! How dare you think that you are loving with the love of my Son, when you love with sacrificial love only one day out of 365! If you truly are my disciples, you will be involved with these people 365 days a year!"

This was a scary thought. But as the congregation began to apply this love on a regular basis, Slaughter writes, "Renewal broke out at our church when the people began actively to do what we had been reading in God's written Word. Jesus was taking us past the information to the place of transformation" (*Spiritual Entrepreneurs*, pp. 55-56).

Let's follow the path along with this prayer:

- love prods us to obedience
- obedience awakens insight
- insight sharpens awareness
- awareness hones discernment
- discernment calls for grace
- grace enables love to grow
- love creates true singleness of mind
- true singleness of mind leads to true righteousness

By way of contrast, in one congregation I pastored there was a man who had not been to church for many years because he disagreed with the choice of furnace the church had made. When he stands before God on the day of judgment, under the purity of God's Son-light, how valid, blameless, pure and righteous will that behavior seem? What hope of transformation is there in that man's life?

"Oh, you refused to honor Me publicly on the Lord's day because your church bought an oil burning furnace instead of gas?" Disobedience leads to a dead end.

Know the Truth—Be Set Free

so that you may be able to discern what is best
and may be pure and blameless.

This prayer of Philippians1:9-11—for love that abounds in knowledge, insight and discernment that abounds more and more, for purity, blamelessness and the fruits of righteousness that comes through Jesus Christ—is a call for an appetite for truthfulness.

In her book *Co-dependence*, former psychotherapist, author and lecturer Anne Wilson Shaef says, "An addiction is anything we feel we have to lie about" (p. 21). She later adds, "The function of an addiction is to keep us out of touch with ourselves" (p. 24). Think about your own life. Is there anything you lie about? How much do you eat? How hard do you work? How much do you give? How much do you spend on yourself? What about your judgmental spirit, your bigotry? Are you truthful about your consumption of substances, alcohol, or drugs? To whom are you lying? Is this how you remain blameless?

Addictive behavior is part of a larger desire to feel in control of ourselves. Like drinking saltwater to quench our thirst, addictive behaviors eventually leave us thirsty. One of the most common addictive behaviors that Christian men lie about is the use of pornography. It has been described as "omnipresent" in our society. How many Christian men remain lukewarm, shallow, defeated, and ineffective as a Christian witness because of defeat in this area? Maybe it's just as well not to know.

One of the ways I have tried to handle this area of my own life is to be honest about the temptation with my wife and a small group of men. Lust has at its heart a longing for control, and pornography becomes a slippery slope as grosser and grosser images are required in order to experience the same hormonal rush of power and pleasure. Being truthful with oneself and with at least one other significant person can keep you accountable. The ultimate answer is to be governed by agape, Christ-filled love. Such love offers healthful power rather than the need for control. This is at the heart of real righteousness.

Radio commentator Paul Harvey tells the grisly story of an Eskimo killing a wolf. It offers insight into the self-destructive nature of lust.

> First the Eskimo coats his knife blade with animal blood and allows it to freeze. Then he adds another layer of blood and another until the blade is completely concealed by frozen blood. Next the hunter fixes his knife in the ground with the blade up. When a wolf follows his sensitive nose to the source of the scent and discovers the bait, he licks it,

tasting the fresh-frozen blood. He begins to lick faster, more and more vigorously, lapping the blade until the keen edge is bare. Feverishly now, harder and harder the wolf licks the blade in the Arctic night. So great becomes his craving for blood that the wolf does not notice the razor sharp sting of the naked blade on his tongue nor does he recognize the instant at which his insatiable thirst is being satisfied by his own warm blood. His carnivorous appetite just craves more—until the dawn finds him dead in the snow (*Leadership*, Winter, 1987, Vol. VIII, No. 1, p. 41).

Preoccupation with oneself is fatal. Insight into oneself and the love of God is a dynamic antidote for self-hypnotic lust.

Recently, I talked to a man who had sat on his church's pulpit committee. Since he had just participated in a nationwide search for a pastor for his large congregation, I asked him what qualities he looked for in such a person. Expecting "outstanding preaching" or "strong administrative gifts" as likely answers, I was surprised when he said, "I want a pastor who is a real person."

What is a "real" person? He/she is the kind of person for whom Paul's prayer is answered. A real person abounds in knowledge and depth of insight; a real person has discernment where phoniness is concerned. A real person understands that true righteousness and purity are the fruit of a relationship with the saving God of the Bible. A real person humbly understands his own human weaknesses and limits and the joy of wholeness through the grace of God.

Paul's heart was an open book. "God can testify how I long for all of you with the affection of Christ Jesus." In that affection he prays not just for knowledge or insight or discernment or purity or righteousness. With the affection of Jesus he cries out for love, agape love, for this congregation. Knowledge, insight, discernment, purity and righteousness focused on the cross amount to more than human power and ability. They are reflections of the Incarnation. As such they bring reality into focus and help people like us become real as we live in the affection of our Lord.

Recently I preached in a church that had only lately come near to closing. I learned that the crisis point involved the long-time choir director and his wife. Few people knew he had been abusive until he shot her and then himself. Standing next to a Christmas tree in the sanctuary as I heard the story, I felt a moment of the *splangkna* of God. How the Lord must have observed this injured life and longed with infinite love to bring healing and maturity and wisdom! Some stronghold of self-hate had fed an unwilling spirit and the compassion of God, which saves when accepted, was held at bay.

Do you suppose God would like to answer Paul's prayer in your life? Remaining in our Lord's affection is not a spiritual luxury. It is at the heart of our salvation.

Questions for Discussion

1. Why do we believe that God in Christ is compassionate? How does that make a difference in our lives?

2. Why do we resist the compassion of Jesus?

3. When was the last time the church you attend made a significant change? Why is change challenging?

4. What is the difference between a tourist and a citizen in the kingdom of God? Which are you?

5. What are some of the basic steps a human being usually takes in growing from childhood to mature adulthood? What are some of the basic steps Christians take in moving from forgiveness to discipleship?

6. Someone has said that nothing can kill the self, not even hell. If that is so, what are we to do with our "selves" as children of God?

7. Transformation comes at a price. Does that mean we have to earn it? If not, what does it mean?

8. Lies are spiritual red flags, simple though they may seem. Where are you dishonest or in denial in some way? Why?

9. Why is an accountability partner or group an important resource in living a Christian life?

10. Whom do you consider a "real" person? What traits or behaviors identify them as such?

CHAPTER FIVE

Holding on to Joy: Reaching out for Real Success

Philippians 1:21-26
For me to live is Christ and to die is gain.
If I am to go on living in the body,
this will mean fruitful labor for me.
Yet what shall I choose? I do not know! I am torn between the two:
I desire to depart and be with Christ, which is better by far;
but it is more necessary for you that I remain in the body.
Convinced of this, I know that I will remain,
and I will continue with all of you for your progress and joy in the faith,
so that through my being with you again, your joy in Christ Jesus will
overflow on account of me.

Are you a success? I seriously considered this question some years ago when I talked with a parishioner who trains sales people for a major corporation.

"Most people do not succeed in life," he said, " because they have not decided what success really means to them. Consequently, they never know when they have achieved it."

This sounds like a line from a motivational speech. And yes, it could lead down a trail of superficial, self-centered conclusions.

But it doesn't have to.

A clear idea of success didn't adversely affect Jesus. His life illustrates that success does not need to be limited to the bottom line of a profit and loss sheet.

So, what is success?

One day during my college years a friend was stopped by a zealous student who had transferred from a very conservative Bible college. He aggressively asked my friend a success-type question:

"Do you know who you are, and do you know where you're going?"

My friend's reply was immediate, "I'm Jim Sharp, and I'm going to Johnson Main dormitory."

Obviously, Jim thought it the sort of question that deserved a foolish answer.

"Do you know who you are and do you know where you're going?" is, as my children say, "cheesy." It seems to call for a cheesy answer. So let's try a different "success" question.

What do you claim are the most important things in your life, and what have you done in the last 30 days that validates that claim?

If your claim and your activities are in harmony, it is likely you can be considered successful. The worthiness of what you value most would, in one way or another, qualify the significance of your success.

Speaking of what he valued most, the apostle Paul wrote, "For to me, to live is Christ and to die is gain" (1:21). That could be as cheesy as a Wisconsin warehouse were it not for Paul's faithful walk and the eternal worth of his desires. His outstretched hands were clearly consistent in reaching for this kind of success.

He was pro-Jesus and proactive.

For me to live is Christ.

Success is Non-circumstatial

We might paraphrase an oft-noted principle from the book of James and say, "Success without works is dead." Living a successful Christian life requires intentional behaviors of faith. Acting in harmony with our stated Christian values can call for difficult, self-denying choices.

The great temptation for many of us is to live what we might call a maintenance life:

> get by the best you can,
> hold on until the weekend,
> do what has to be done to survive,
> and hope there's a little left over for yourself.

Life can feel like the playground ride that spun so fast you were afraid to jump off.

Our energy is instinctively invested in two words: HOLD ON!

However, the fundamental flaw in a maintenance-type life is this: it is *re-active* driven rather than *pro-active*. Its motivation is external, rather than internal. This sets the stage for unhappiness and a "feeling" of failure because one's true, inner longings are constantly frustrated by the demands of others or circumstances.

Pastor and author Jamie Buckingham wrote about a man named Harry Gasque who personified the problem-driven lifestyle. Harry was a wanderer. About twice a year he traveled through the South Carolina town where Jamie pastored a church. One spring morning Harry stopped to chat. He was headed north to Asheville, North Carolina, or so he said. Later that day Jamie saw Harry hitchhiking south.

"I thought you were going north," Jamie called out to him.

"Well," he said, spitting a stream of tobacco juice on the sidewalk, "it seems most of the traffic is headed south. So I crossed the road and decided to head down to Augusta instead" (*The Last Word*, Jamie Buckingham, pp. 25-26, Logos, 1978).

Now this may not be a bad method of operation for a wanderer. But Christians are not wanderers. We are pilgrims. We have been told to seek something—the kingdom of God. That goal is intentionally vast to allow for God's unique plan in every life within the bigger picture of universal kingdom truths. It is a command that calls for a pro-active attitude in order to achieve success. It is a call that demands a divine presence, providing guidance and power. When Paul declared, "For me to live is Christ," he was testifying to living a Person-driven, Person-enabled life.

What also often happens is this: Functionally, we live like wanderers, living in subjection to the pressures of the traffic around us rather than the values, the Presence within us. Consequently, we can be "successful" in our basic coping skills but still feel like failures.

Surely Paul understood such external pressures when he wrote Romans 12:2, "Do not conform any longer to the pattern of this world, but be transformed by the renewing of your mind. Then you will be able to test and approve what God's will is—his good, pleasing and perfect will." Being saved, but not pressing on to inner transformation, and sitting on hands that should be outstretched is a prescription for unhappiness. Yet this is an all-too-common spiritual posture of many Christians.

Seminary professor and author Howard Hendrix was talking to a parishioner one day and he asked her, "How are you doing, Sister?" With a holy limp in her voice she answered, "Pretty well, under the circumstances." He replied, "What are you doing under there!"

Isn't that where a lot of us live, under the circumstances? We are too often problem-driven or pleasure-driven rather than Person-driven.

Somewhere along his faith journey, Paul had obviously moved from domination by circumstantial, external influences. We can deduce this from Paul's clear and enviable testimony, "I have learned to be content whatever the circumstances. I know what it is to be in need, and I know what it is to have plenty. I have learned the secret of being content in any and every situation . . . " (Phil. 4:11-12).

We should note that what Paul meant here by being content is not hedonistic, self-indulgent gratification. How do we know? We know because self-gratifying contentment is always directly tied to the circumstances. When "the kids leave home and the dog dies" is a popular formula for *contentment*. We must see with absolute clarity that success should *not be circumstantial.* It is not built around *what* is but rather *Who* is.

"For me to live is comfortable circumstances." *Not!*

"For me to live is Christ, and to die (to move from seeing in a mirror dimly to seeing face to face, to move from knowing in part to knowing fully) is gain."

The Paradox of Humble Success

for me to live is Christ

Consider the challenging path to success alluded to in James 4:7-10: "Submit yourselves, then, to God. Resist the devil, and he will flee from you. Come near to God and he will come near to you. Wash your hands, you sinners, and purify your hearts, you double-minded. Grieve, mourn, and wail. Change your laughter to mourning and your joy to gloom. Humble yourselves before the Lord, and he will lift you up."

To move from saying, "For me to live is ME," to "for me to live is Christ," is an awesome transformation of the heart. It means a daily dying to circumstantial satisfaction/success. It means grief. Philippians 2 offers welcome encouragement, ". . . continue to work out your salvation with fear and trembling, for it is God who works in you to will and to act according to his good pleasure" (2:12b, 13). Continue to stretch out your hands in faith, for the Lord is already reaching out to you. This change of heart is not a unilateral effort. God is in the yoke with us. ". . . he will lift you up," James affirms. It is our responsibility to humble ourselves in faith.

In our efforts to seek such transformation, anxiety, self-reflection and evaluation can easily be mistaken and substituted for humble surrender. (How many times a day do you say the word "I" to yourself?) After all, who wants to grieve, mourn and wail? Who wants to humble himself before the Lord? Socrates' advice to "know thyself" sounds much more empowering! Later in Paul's letter, he strongly declares that his great desire was not to know *himself*, but to know *Jesus Christ*. And, yes, that meant "becoming like him in his death," finding success beyond immediate circumstances.

It is fascinating to recall Freud's observations about Nietzsche, the famous atheist philosopher, who knew himself better than any other human being Freud had known. It is fascinating because Nietzsche spent the last 11 years of his life insane. Transformation includes self-knowledge. But self-knowledge apart from God-knowledge (grace-knowledge) is like having a motorcycle on a cruise ship in the middle of the ocean. You can drive it all around your little world, but it will never get you anywhere.

In 2 Corinthians 3 we read that there is a kind of spiritual blindness intrinsic to the human heart. Verse 16 declares, " . . . whenever anyone turns to the Lord, the veil is taken away." We can discover freedom to see ourselves, to see the deceitfulness and emptiness of our hearts, but not through intense introspection. Christian freedom is found in humble surrender to and spiritual unity with the living Savior. 2 Corinthians 3 concludes with the wonderful hope that Christian believers " . . . are being transformed into [Jesus'] likeness, with ever-increasing glory, which comes from the Lord, who is the Spirit."

Success is an Inside Job

Student of psychology and author Keith Miller offers an interesting view of human nature and the veil that hides the truth. In his book *The Secret Life of the Soul*, he describes how fallen human nature creates what he terms "the constructed personality" (pp. 59ff). He imagines a home video of a boy named Billy on Easter morning. The weather in Billy's town has been rainy, but Easter morning is clear. Billy, dressed in his pristine Easter outfit, begs to go outside. Finally, his mother gives in, warning him to stay out of the mud. Once outside, Billy gets together with neighbor, Bobby. He invites Bobby to view his own reflection in a puddle, and, as Bobby leans over for a look, Billy pushes him into the dirty water. As Bobby cries in protest, the mothers of both boys emerge from their homes. Billy's mother asks, "Billy, did you push Bobby?" Keith Miller writes, "Up to now Billy has never lied because he thinks his mother can read his mind." But thinking he will get walloped anyway, he pleads innocent. Then the miracle happens: she believes him! It is a crossroads for Billy, his initiation into a life of duplicity. Internal division, the construction of a false self, Miller says, begins.

I cannot say whether Keith Miller's picture of this process is accurate or not, but I find it thought-provoking. It may speak to the evolution by which "double-mindedness" (James 1:8) comes to hold sway in our lives. Later in *The Secret Life of the Soul*, Miller declares, "Psychologists have long known that our secrets control us" (p. 182). That is a possibility worth pondering. It strongly suggests that the path to wholeness, out of double-mindedness, is a path into truth and reality. Paul would say this is the path we take as we seek to live "in Christ." So to say, "for me to live is Christ," is to declare a conscious intention to escape the shadow of secrets, two-mindedness, and to walk in the light.

Isn't this at the core of the power of twelve-step groups, the essence of the evangelical "altar call," and the basic implication of the call to repent and believe the gospel? A life in Christ is a life in perpetual repentance, turning from secrets and lies to reality. Miller observes,

> I saw that my soul's imprisonment had seriously impaired my connection with reality, my integrity—because of the denial, control, and projection of my constructed personality. I wasn't sure I could tell when I was deceiving myself or other people. But I was sure that I didn't want to do it any more.
>
> For me, finding healing involved two essential elements. *First*, I had to find a place where I could see integrity in action, where it was safe to risk being open. I needed a context in which I could tell my own truth as I discovered it, and where I could test my new trust in God. *Second*, I had to learn to

see the specific nature and extent of my *unreality* so that my authenticity could be reestablished (p. 178).

Anyone who cares about vitality in the church should want ears to hear these words. Christian fellowships ought to be places where integrity (consistency between stated purposes and goals and actual behavior) is witnessed. If we are to understand our opaqueness, our denial, our secrets and lies, we will be greatly helped by people who are working on transparency. This was central to the impact of the early days of the Lay Witness Mission movement. Teams of lay persons would spend a weekend visiting a local church, sharing their stories. Sometimes the candor of confessions was so surprising that the movement was criticized for spiritual exhibitionism. Often, however, the honesty of the witnesses opened the floodgates of a congregation for an inflow of veil-lifting grace and truth. The Alcoholics Anonymous principle, "we are as sick as our secrets," is a challenge to seek freedom in the truth.

Let's pause a moment and be as candid as possible. How would you fill in the blank, "for me to live is _____?"

The more honestly we can answer that question, the more fully the veil that hides truth and obscures freedom can be removed. This is a "fear and trembling," "grieving, mourning and wailing" process. But it is crucial to understand one thing. Paul did not say, "For me to live is to grieve and mourn and wail over myself." He said, "For me to live is Christ." This is the meaning of John 14:6a, "*I* am the way and the truth and the life," and the implication of 2 Corinthians 3:16, "But whenever anyone turns *to the Lord* [emphasis mine], the veil is taken away." ". . . in view of God's mercy [in view of Jesus] "offer your bodies as living sacrifices" (Romans 12:1). The author of Hebrews had this in mind when he wrote, ". . . let us throw off everything that hinders. . . . Let us fix our eyes on Jesus. . ." (Hebrews 12:1b, 2a). He is the truth who sets us free to live truly successful lives. Our key task as believers is to abide in him. Theologian Emile Cailliet noted that as Jesus approached the cross, he gave his disciples the secret of victorious living in the image of the vine and the branches. The word *abide* appears four times in John 15:4. Cailliet writes, "The sense of our utter, personal dependence on the Presence as *Thou to me*, and I to Thee must become what Plutarch called 'a long-standing habit.' It must be our second nature, if we are finally to recover our true nature" (*Journey into Light*, p. 104).

Fyodor Dostoeyski, was a man who was long-experienced in the ways of the world. Then a brush with death awakened him to the fragility of life. Ten subsequent years in hard labor, having only a New Testament to read and mixed with the company of all manner of human debris, left him with this conviction, "If anyone proved to me that Christ was outside the truth . . . then I would prefer to remain with Christ than with the truth." Dostoeyski understood that our secrets, our deep biases can temper truth. When he met Christ, he encountered Someone beyond such relativity. In Dostoeyski's novel *The Brothers Karamazov*, the devout Alyosha, brother to cynical Ivan, says, "I do not know the answer to the problem of evil, but I do know love." The author of those words had met transparent Love. Authentic life and Christ were one and the same. Consequently, to abide in him is to encounter authentic life.

John Wesley constructed an entire sermon around the concept of a "house of religion." The porch was repentance. The door was justification. The rest of the house was sanctification. It is our task to give Jesus permission to occupy every nook and cranny of the house. He may knock on the door of a favorite room, the room of lust or ambition or control, for many years. We stand on the other side of the door in fear and trembling. Can we handle it if we let him in? Will it kill us? Will we lose control?

Success comes not from "getting our house in order." That only serves to feed our neurotic needs for control. Stability and all the fruit of the Spirit come from letting Jesus be at home in every room. It is truly an inside job: "Christ in you, the hope of glory" (Colossians 1:27).

The Truth Gives You Choices

for me to live is Christ

We witness this hope blossoming forth as the disciples tarry together between the Ascension and Pentecost. What was going on in that upper room? The "veil" was removed by the loving power of the blood of Christ. The now risen Lord was knocking on the door of their hearts as never before. A great spiritual paradigm shift was taking place. By the grace of the Lamb of God, the Holy Spirit had a new freedom to convict and convince. Confronted by truth in the power of the Holy Spirit, the disciples were given opportunity to become more responsible children of God. In chapter two of this letter to the church in Philippi we can read of this new kind of spiritual formation made possible by receiving the "mind of Christ," a paradigm, a vision of life that can remove the veil of self-motivated and self-focused religion.

Fear and *trembling* are realistic terms to characterize a human journey into transformation. Just as it is common for individuals undergoing psychotherapy to bail out rather than undergo the pain of honesty and change, so it can be for Christians. Scott Peck in *The Road Less Traveled* described the nature of original or basic sin as "laziness." This was not intended to imply slothfulness. He was noting the usual passive resistance to the work of change observable in the process of therapy.

When Adam and Eve committed the "original sin," they also promptly employed the original crutch. They took the role of a victim, Adam claiming victimization by Eve, and Eve pointing her finger at the snake. This was akin to saying, "For me to live is the responsibility of something beyond my true self." I say *true self*, for quite often we blame, not only others or our circumstances, but also our weak self for the failures of what we think of as our real or best self.

In Stephen Covey's bestseller, *The 7 Habits of Highly Effective*

People, he includes one sentence that is worth more than the price of the book. He puts his finger on why it is unhealthful to live with the attitude of a victim: "Our behavior is a function of our decisions, not our conditions" (p. 71).

A victim is a person who lives *conditionally*. Remember the earlier observation in this chapter that real success is not conditional. True success is the result of healthful decisions that may, often as not, be made in spite of conditions rather than because of them. These cross-bearing choices that bring freedom will generally spring from walking in the truth, abiding in the truth, finding grace to overcome our passive resistance to the work of repentance.

Dennis Kinlaw tells the story of two spiritual giants of an earlier generation, Samuel Chadwick and G. Campbell Morgan. Both men were invited to speak at the same conference. G. Campbell Morgan was well established as a great Bible teacher. Samuel Chadwick was honored to be on the same program.

"Perhaps folks are taking notice of me!" he thought.

Each morning they both preached at successive hours, alternating the first and second position. The first morning both men preached to large crowds. The next day Morgan preached first to a large number. When his sermon was over, a sizable group took their leave. The next morning Chadwick spoke to a small crowd and then watched as the room filled up for Morgan's message. It was painful to the young preacher. He went to his room and knelt in prayer.

> This is not fair, Lord.
> Oh, what do you want me to do about it?
> Well, I don't know. But it hurts. It's embarrassing.
> Chadwick was not prepared for the Lord's response.
> Are you sorry, Chadwick, that we've got a fellow like
> Morgan on our team?
> No! But it hurts.
> Are you suggesting that I quit blessing Morgan?

From that point on through the rest of the conference Samuel Chadwick set aside a time to pray for G. Campbell Morgan. "After that," he said, "I found myself going with excitement to hear Morgan each day, giving thanks that we had a fellow like that on our team" (*Preaching in the Spirit*, D. Kinlaw, pp. 103-5). Which of those men left that conference a success? We trust Morgan did. We know Chadwick did!

Chadwick dealt with a core value of his life: why he was a preacher. Was it for acclaim? Was it for Christ and with Christ? That is the kind of paradigm shift Paul had experienced, and every believer should seek. As the veil is removed from our hearts and our true desires, our core values are exposed, we have, by grace, the choice of choosing a higher reason for living and a Living Presence with Whom to bond. "For me to live [pro-actively] is Christ."

for me to live is Christ

Victor Frankl learned about the power that comes from laying aside the "original crutch" in the prison camps of Nazi Germany. When all else was taken from him, he discovered a gracious gift of God: the power to decide how he would respond to his circumstances. He found the power latent in choosing not to live as a victim. Frankl became a classic example of the truth of Covey's principle—our behavior is a function of our decisions, not our conditions.

As we view Jesus on the cross, we observe this principle at its zenith. Just about everyone in the story acts like a victim. Jesus is passed from Annas to Caiaphas who passes him on to Pilate. Pilate, having admitted that Jesus had committed no crime worthy of death, caves in to the crowd. On the cross, one of the thieves mocks Jesus. The other thief does an amazing thing. He removes the veil of the victim and takes responsibility for himself (Luke 23:40-42). There, in the midst of the confusion and apparent tragedy of the moment, a person who refuses the victim's role and stretches out his spiritual hands finds grace. Jesus promises him a place in paradise.

But the one person who seemed most conclusively to be a victim, Jesus, rejects that attitude. We find the reason why in John 10:17-18 where Jesus says, "The reason my Father loves me is that I lay down my life—only to take it up again. No one takes it from me, but I lay it down *of my own accord*" [emphasis mine].

Jesus himself said, ". . . whoever loses his life for my sake will find it" (Matthew 10:39b). Obviously this was not cheap talk. Jesus had lost his life for the Father's sake, with the Father as his only supporter, and he had found it in so doing. Power came, not in self-understanding, but in self-surrender. There was a room in Jesus' house called "obedience unto death." When the Father knocked, Jesus let Him in.

One of the most thought-provoking books I have ever read is William Glasser's *Take Effective Control of Your Life*. Glasser looks at three of the most basic components of life: feeling, thinking and doing. He observes that of the three we have the least control over what we feel. We have some control over what we think. But of the three, we have the most control over what we do. In the Garden of Gethsemene, Jesus was full of fear. He could not avoid the thought that the Father might let this cup pass, but what mattered was that he chose to lose his life.

This brings us back to where we began—choosing to live a purpose-driven (ultimately, Person-driven) rather than a problem-centered life. What happens to a Christian who decides to attempt this?

We find ourselves faced repeatedly with a fundamental choice: whom will I be like, Judas or Peter?

Where Should Our Despair Lead Us?

Both of these men discovered that their core values were much more self-serving than they thought at first. Both failed. One took his life. One went back to Jesus with outstretched hands, realizing his need for him. It wouldn't be the last time Peter's core values were challenged and, in time, transformed as another dimension of the veil was removed (see Galatians 2:11-21). We could say that Judas took responsibility for himself in his self-execution. He lost his life, didn't he? And it dramatically affirms the importance of believing and living "for me to live is *Christ*." Jesus said, "whoever loses his life *for my sake* will find it" (Matthew 10:39 [emphasis mine]).

Beyond our feelings and thoughts and power of choice is our heart, that center of self-consciousness where our core values abide, where the veil stubbornly resists removal. 1 Corinthians 13 tells us the startling truth that we can be spiritually gifted and sacrificially proactive and still need a transformation of our heart.

Henry Cloud and John Townsend's book *False Assumptions* offers wise advice about some of the myths common to spiritually minded people. One of the chapters, "If I Make the Right Choices I Will Grow Spiritually," addresses the misconception that acting on good intentions will make Christians grow in their faith. While the authors point out the importance of making choices, they go a step further and recognize that the ultimate motivator behind choices is one's heart. They shed light on growing in grace, noting the difference between a *right* intention and a *pure* intention.

A *right* intention is the choice to do the right thing. A *pure* intention is wanting what we have chosen. They write, "In the biblical sense this is what it truly means 'to will.' The words most often translated 'to will' actually mean 'to desire.' *For this reason, to think of an act of the will apart from a pure heart that desires the things God desires is unbiblical* (italics theirs). God wants us to will and want the same things that he wants" (p. 172).

They go on to suggest the following list of choices we may make that the Holy Spirit can use in the process of transforming our hearts.

•Confess our sins
•Give up the notion that we can save ourselves
•Submit our inability to God

•Ask for help in searching for our faults
•Repent
•Take account of our needs and let others meet them
•Make amends
•Forgive
•Invest and practice talents
•Seek God
•Seek truth
•Love one another

These are choices—acts of will—that can serve as catalysts to spiritual growth, transforming our hearts and our true desires, implanting more of the mind of Christ. They call for removing any and all of the veil that separates us from God's gracious will and purposes.

There is an old Spanish proverb that says habits begin like the threads of a spider's web, but in the end they turn into ropes. Many of those ropes become knotted and very difficult to undo. This is the predicament Christians face along with everyone else. We begin with a divided heart scarred by rebellion. We grow up in a fallen world, where our instincts and the routine struggles of life weave together to form strong ropes of attitude and action. Some of these are quite contrary to God's Spirit. The explosion in the number of 12-step groups in recent years affirms the widespread recognition of our enslavement to such strong ropes.

Therapist Alan Wheelis describes the discouragement that attempts at change inevitably bring,

> More often the course upon which one has embarked entails so much anxiety, uncertainty, confusion, that reappraisal becomes necessary. One finds that his entire self was not known, that submerged aspects of self now rise up in terror, threat, and subversion, screaming outrage, demanding revocation. One is forced to a halt, sometimes driven back.

The whole issue has to be rethought. "What I am giving up is more important than I knew. Maybe I don't want to change. Am I going the wrong way?" (*How People Change*, p. 107). At such times we can react like Judas or like Peter. Grace gives us the choice.

E. Stanley Jones writes along a similar vein when he says,

Into the conscious mind is introduced by conversion a new sense of conscious cleanness, a new loyalty, a new love. This introduction is so real, so satisfying, so conduct-determining, that the converted think the battle is over, that life is now to be one glad song of victory. Those honeymoon days come to an end, usually within a year. The subconscious urges, which have been lying low, apparently stunned into insensibility by the introduction of this new and different and authoritative life in the conscious mind, now begin to reassert themselves. Tempers, moods, fears, resentments, which we thought were gone forever, now lift their heads from the storm cellars of the subconscious, and the struggle between the conscious and the subconscious ensues (*Conversion*, p. 229).

From what we know of the lives of Peter and Judas, both men seemed likely candidates for serious inner conflicts. In both cases, Jesus clearly understood their infirmities before they failed him. It is tempting to suggest possible reasons for their varying responses to failure. Such possibilities would only be speculation. What is best said is this: Choose what Peter chose. Keep going back to Jesus. In so doing we give him continued access to our hearts for his continuing work of transformation. Swiss author and counselor Paul Tournier notes, "The price that has to be paid for finding truly personal life is a very high one. It is a price in terms of the acceptance of responsibility. And the awareness of responsibility inevitably leads either to despair or to confession and grace. More is needed than the good intentions of the humanist. What is required is a new outlook, a personal revolution, a miracle" (*The Meaning of Persons*, p. 158). The living Christ makes such miracles possible. Miracles do happen. Paradigm shifts happen every day, some of them deep within and under the assistance of grace.

Amazing Grace—How Sweet the Sound

for me to live is Christ

Charles' Dickens' classic story *A Christmas Carol* presents us with a universal character, Scrooge, who is forced to face himself and take responsibility for his actions. With supernatural assistance, he illustrates what Tournier observes when he says, "That is what living means—jumping over the hedges of the personage that have naturally grown up and hemmed us in" (*The Meaning of Persons*, p. 205). Grace is there—Jesus is there—to forgive and to help us jump over our own shadows.

The apostle Paul awakened to a revelation: the only people who live are people who live by grace. Jesus is the source of that grace.

As a person seeking to follow Jesus, my understanding and internalization of these truths has been incremental and usually painful.

After nine years of full-time ministry, I hit the wall. I awakened one day and was emotionally dead—no tears, no laughter. It scared me. I called a trusted counselor 500 miles away and made an appointment. As part of that trip I visited my one surviving grandparent, an Alzheimer's patient. I also went to visit my brother's grave. I hoped that my counseling visit would result in a healing miracle. What I really wanted was to be so whole and complete that I would never suffer emotional pain again. Of course, it didn't happen. Essentially, the counselor listened to my story, empathized from his own experience, and then asked,

"Did God call you into the ministry?"

"Yes. It is one reality in my life about which I have no doubt."

"Then you are his problem," he said "and he will take care of you. You must trust him."

The counselor went to the heart of the matter, to my heart and to God's heart. I had been doing the right thing, but I had been doing it with the wrong desire/will/heart. For me to live had not been Christ, my grace-based love relationship with him. It had been self-satisfying success based on observable achievement. I wanted to be God's answer for the church that I was serving. God wanted me to be his problem, or in the positive sense, his opportunity to live through me.

Not long after that I was driving to an out-of-town hospital one morning when I heard Dr. James Kennedy on the radio. He preached a sermon entitled "The Secret of Commitment." It was about the life of missionary and explorer David Livingstone. The secret was a verse of Scripture that was the basis of Livingstone's amazing life, Matthew 28:20, "I am with you always." For him to live was the knowledge of Christ with him. It was a truth that purified his life and brought him success in the midst of a life abundant in awesome trials and heartbreaks.

He lived by grace. Jesus was the source of that grace. I had to believe that. When God calls us, as he does all believers, he allows us to become his problem, his opportunity. If only Judas had seen that.

To live is to go back to him, over and over and over forever; to keep our hands outstretched toward him. Of course, to die is gain. The struggle to live above the victim's role, to cope with one's contradictory tendencies, to follow the Way, is a landscape dotted with beautiful moments of faithfulness and blessing, as well as ugly craters of sin. Certainly to walk on the landscape of eternity will be gain, and then some. But in the meantime, blessed is the person who can say, "For me to live is Christ." Such a person, seeking the mind of Christ by grace, can claim the prophesy of Ezekiel 36:25-27 "I will sprinkle clean water on you, and you will be clean; I will cleanse you from all your impurities and from all your idols. I will

give you a new heart and put a new spirit in you; I will remove
from you your heart of stone and give you a heart of flesh. And I
will put my Spirit in you and move you to follow my decrees and
be careful to keep my laws."

To live like this is to live in Christ; it is a PERSON-(the Person
of Jesus Christ) driven life, and that is true success.

Questions for Discussion

1. How have you been defining success? Are you satisfied with your
   definition?

2. What do you normally consider to be the most important
   concerns of your life, your real priorities? Do your actions reflect
   those priorities? Where might you repent, turn toward walking
   what you talk (even what you tell yourself)?

3. What does it mean "to be willing to be made willing" to yield
   to God?

4. Why is self-knowledge limited in its impact in being transformed
   as Christians?

5. How do our secrets exert control over us? How do we escape
   such bonds?

6. How do you fill in the "for me to live is _____"
   blank?

7. Why is it not enough to say, "for me to live is to be honest with
   myself"?

8. Are you aware right now of rooms in your "house" or closets or drawers where Jesus does not have access?

9. Where in your life do you see yourself as a victim? Does it enrich your life to feel this way? How can you escape victimhood through faith in God?

10. What crises of faith have helped you grow in grace and in the knowledge of Jesus Christ?

CHAPTER SIX

Hands Outstretched to Unseen Love

Philippians 2:1-4
If you have any encouragement from being united with Christ,
if any comfort from his love, if any fellowship with the Spirit,
if any tenderness and compassion,
then make my joy complete by being like-minded,
having the same love, being one in spirit and purpose.
Do nothing out of selfish ambition or vain conceit,
but in humility consider others better than yourselves.
Each of you should look not only to your own interests,
but also to the interests of others.

During the spring of my final year of seminary, I was serving two churches in southern Indiana just across the river from Louisville, Kentucky. One April day I watched churning funnel clouds rip through the heart of that city. Later, as the extent of the damage became painfully clear, the destruction in one area of town was especially heartbreaking. Cherokee Park was a city treasure, a landscape richly dotted with magnificent old trees. There would be no quick fix for this sudden loss.

Amazingly, many of the downed trees quickly began to show new buds. The extent of the damage slowed down the progress of cleanup efforts to the point that this forest of unearthed trunks and broken limbs actually burst forth in full leaves. To look at the park as spring unfolded, it appeared that the damage was not so severe as first believed. But appearances can be deceiving. Before long the buds and leaves nourished by stored up nutrients could not be sustained independent of a continuing source and they slowly starved to death.

As we look back at the beginning of Paul's letter to the Philippians, we see definite signs of life—vibrant green leaves invigorated by a source no storm can destroy:

thanksgiving
prayer
faith
hope in spite of opposition
joy

This kind of spiritual foliage means there are roots drawing vitality from an unseen source, "the *help* given by the Spirit of Jesus Christ" (1:19). Moving into chapter two, the kind of help we can expect moves from theory to practice. Imagine interstate-sized billboards situated around your church on which are placarded these phrases:

Make Jesus' joy complete by having his love
Make Jesus' joy complete by being in one mind
Do nothing from selfish ambition
Do nothing out of selfish conceit
In humility regard others as better than yourselves
Look not to your own interests
Look to the interests of others

In 2:1-4 we are reminded why the Christian life is a high calling and why all who follow it will need help given by the Spirit of Jesus Christ.

As a United Methodist district superintendent, the memory of my first involvement on the inside of pastoral assignments (appointments, we call them) is still as fresh as yesterday. I was reminded that "regarding others as better than oneself" and "looking not to one's own interests" take a great deal of help for those expecting to move to a new church. One pastor, who was especially unhappy with his new appointment, complained bitterly that the system was "tragically" broken, with some pastors seeming to move to larger, more lucrative churches regardless of performance or fruitfulness. As I listened, I was aware that while our method is far from perfect, one of its most tragic flaws was the kind of comparisons that this pastor was drawing. (When I talk to people in other systems of pastoral assignment, it seems this flaw is common to all.) How far from Philippians 2!

Not much in Philippians 2 frets over how fair life may be. Concern for fairness is a manifestation of pride. Most of us need help to rise above such fretting. But the irony is this: moving beyond pride calls for more than strength of will. If willpower overcame self-focus we would inevitably end up proud of our willpower. The antidote must be of a different kind. As providence would have it, "the help given by the Spirit of Jesus Christ" is of a different kind. It is love—agape—an attitude defined by Jesus' response to the call to the cross. It is a source of life as evergreen as Jesus' resurrection.

God's Love: Fertility Personified

Agape (God's kind of love) is the wellspring of the Christian faith that nourishes those who put their trust in God through his grace in Jesus. The author of the letter to the Hebrews was attempting to affirm this qualitative difference between God as power and God as personal, nourishing love when he wrote about Jesus, saying, "For we do not have a high priest who is unable to sympathize with our weaknesses, but we have one who has been tempted in every way, just as we are—yet was without sin. Let us then approach the throne of grace with confidence, so that we may receive mercy and find grace to help us in our time of need" (4:15-16). The "help given by the Spirit of Jesus Christ" is not only power, but nourishing, personal love. (Part of the reason the Spirit led Paul to write letters to churches was to give guidance and encouragement to those individuals and communities through whom Jesus intended to live again, through whom he intended to give the "help" of incarnate personal love.)

This is why the help of which Paul writes enables him to have hope that his troubles will produce fruit. He has put down roots in the soil of God, a soil that has as its essence personal, moral, intelligent *agape* love. When Paul writes to the Corinthians and says, ". . . Christ's love compels us" (2 Corinthians 5:14), he is talking about a source of spiritual nourishment that is alive with the personal, loving vitality seen in Jesus' himself.

if any comfort from his love

I grew up in Indiana where it seemed to me in late spring you could open the window, throw out some tomato seeds and weeks later begin harvesting beautiful, delicious tomatoes. That rich soil *compelled* health and growth by virtue of its inherently nourishing nature. The love of God expressed through Jesus and available to us through the Holy Spirit (Romans 5:5) is a compelling force and source. And we have been designed by God to seek that force. Paul did this and the result was "comfort" (2:1). Comfort comes from root words meaning "with strength." The *comfort* of the love of God through Jesus abides in the lives of those whose fruitfulness can be explained only by his presence.

The Cosmic Influence: Our Image of God

if you have any encouragement from being united with Christ

This source is the necessary and more-than-human strength Jesus had in mind in John 15 when he spoke of himself as the True Vine. So unique, divine and humanly irreplaceable is this source that Jesus flatly says, "Apart from me you can do nothing" (15:5). Becky Pippert's insight in *Hope Has Its Reasons* speaks of this: "Only what transcends us can transform us" (p. 66). Only the transcending *help/comfort* of Jesus enables us to live a life of transformation; that is, an unnatural re-formation of ourselves.

It is clear that Paul had discovered a transcendent, nourishing power and he kept his hands outstretched toward that power, ever drawing life from him Who is the Life. "For me to live is Christ" (1:21).

What is of crucial importance is his discovery that the heartbeat of this necessary and transcendent power is divine love. In John 15 Jesus makes it as clear as he could, directing us "remain in my love" (15:9b). Like Paul, we must keep our spiritual hands outstretched, ever reaching for that love through scripture, prayer, fellowship with others in whom that love abides, and obedient service. Clearly we are stretching our hands out to the richest love ever known. What a difference it makes to reach out to God as described in Jesus Christ in Philippians 2!

Herman Melville, author of *Moby Dick*, once wrote, "The reason the mass of men fear God, and at the bottom dislike Him, is because they rather distrust His heart, and fancy Him all brain like a watch" (*Disappointment With God*, Philip Yancey, p. 54). What we "fancy" God to be like is of all-encompassing importance. A. W. Tozer, in his book on the attributes of God, states,

> What comes into our minds when we think about God is the most important thing about us. The history of mankind will probably show that no people has ever risen above its religion, and man's spiritual history will positively demonstrate that no religion has ever been greater than its idea of God . . . . We tend by a secret law of the soul to move toward our mental image of God" (*The Knowledge of the Holy*, p. 9).

The furor that was created in the late 20th century when attempts were made to "re-image" God was not making mountains out of molehills. Our image of God is at the center of the bull's-eye of our beliefs. At a different end of the theological spectrum from Tozer, contemporary religious thinker, Marcus Borg, in *The God We Never Knew* states flatly, "My central claim is very direct: our concept of God matters" (p.11).

make my joy complete by being like minded

Historian Russell Kirk has observed that the absence of a compelling vision of a divine Other was chief among the causes of the collapse of the brilliant civilization of the classical Greeks.

> It was the clear relativism of the Sophists, not the mystical insights of Plato, nor Aristotle's aspiration after the Supreme Good, which dominated the thinking of the classical Greeks in their decadence. The failure of the Greeks to find an enduring popular religious sanction for the order of civilization has been a main cause of the collapse of the world of the polis (quoted in *Deliver Us From Evil*, R. Zacharias, p. 38).

Tozer is correct. We do move toward our mental image of God. It is not a coincidence that the Greeks, as Kirk points out, were dominated by relativistic thinking. Lack of faith in a transcendent God led to a materialistic pattern of life and inevitable collapse.

With characteristic clarity, Ravi Zacharias illustrates the foolishness of a relativistic worship-any-god-just-worship mindset. He tells of a unique building constructed on the campus of Ohio State University. Called the Wexner Center for the Performing Arts, it was described by *Newsweek* magazine as "America's first deconstructionist building." The exterior was eclectic, a combination of styles. Its interior was even more disconcerting, with pillars hanging from the ceiling, stairways that went nowhere and angled surfaces designed to create a sense of vertigo. The architect, it was reported, had designed the building to reflect life itself—senseless and incoherent.

Having heard the rationale for the building's design, Zacharias had just one question: "Did he do the same with the foundation?" (*Can Man Live Without God?*, p. 21). There are basic elements in life that our wishes and whims may disguise but ultimately cannot ignore.

Jesus: The God of the Old Covenant Becomes Flesh

It's unavoidably true: foundations must transcend trends. The nature of the One toward whom we are stretching our hands is crucial. Paul rose above his natural inclination to focus on the next life (1:21-26) because of the One with whom he wanted others to share that life.

The letter to the Philippians is usually characterized as an epistle of *joy*. And so it is. It is a call to rejoice. The bigger picture of Paul's life and ministry is needed to reveal the soil from which the joy and hope and endurance of this correspondence flows, "the surpassing greatness of knowing Christ Jesus my Lord" (3:8). That soil is the transcending love of God as revealed in Jesus Christ.

Did abiding in Christ mean discontinuity with the Old Testament and the God whose image is revealed therein? Not at all. Acts 24:14 reflects the synergism of Paul's Old and New Testament faith. " . . . I admit that I worship the God of our fathers as a follower of the Way, which they call a sect. I believe everything that agrees with the Law and that is written in the Prophets...." Then in Acts 26:22 he says, "But I have had God's help to this very day, and so I stand here and testify to small and great alike. I am saying nothing beyond what the prophets and Moses said would happen—"

The roots of his faith were cultivated in the soil of the Old Covenant and God who was at the center of that covenant, finding their intended fruition in Jesus. Ephesians 2:20 speaks of the church, ". . . built on the foundation of the apostles and prophets, with Christ Jesus himself as the chief cornerstone." Knowing the Scriptures of the Old Covenant thoroughly, Paul found no incongruence between Yahweh and Jesus. In Jesus, God had acted redemptively to open a "new and living way" (Hebrews 10:20), which dramatically illustrated anew his agape essence.

any comfort from his love

Yahweh's love is clearly revealed in the Old Testament in the book of Ruth, where we encounter the Hebrew word *ga'al, redeemer.* Ruth's *ga'al* is Boaz, her next-of-kin whose marriage to Ruth continues her family line and saves Ruth and her generation from poverty. What a rich picture of God's faithfulness! Boaz, as Ruth's *go'el*, does not solve her problem in a superficial way, with welfare assistance. He enters into a relationship with Ruth, a life-long relationship that brings her real comfort. In *The Gospel According to Job,* Mike Mason notes the deeper meaning of this story.

> While the book of Ruth is very explicit about the sweeping legal implications of Boaz's action, its real focus is on the amazing fortuitousness of the fact that Boaz—this elder, avuncular, bourgeois landowner who, though related to Ruth, has no more reason to take notice of her than to fly to the moon—this man actually falls head over heels in love with a poor and alien peasant girl! He does not marry Ruth out of a sense of social duty, but rather because he passionately loves her and desires her for his wife.
>
> The moral of the story is that this is exactly how our Lord feels toward us. Although there is no reason on earth why the great King of the Universe should look twice at this petty, filthy breed of grasshoppers called mankind, nevertheless He says to us, "You have stolen my heart, my sister, my bride; you have stolen my heart with one glance of your eyes" (Song 4:9). Imagine—we have stolen the heart of God! (pp. 215-16)

Following the Resurrection, as recorded in Luke 24, we find Jesus on the road to Emmaus walking with a couple of downhearted men. "And beginning with Moses and all the Prophets, he explained to them what was said in all the Scriptures concerning himself" (vs. 27). Could it be that those men realized for the first time what Jehovah's love was really like? Is not that ever since what the Holy Spirit has been revealing, as Jesus is lifted up?

We can only imagine the joy Paul felt as he reflected on the Scriptures through the lenses of Jesus. The cataracts of law upon law upon law, added to the Scriptures through centuries of well-meaning rabbis, were removed by the laser-like light of the risen Lord. The implants of truth and grace made visible the love of God, and it was in perfect focus.

We witness a poetic look at the powerful love of God that apprehended Paul through Jesus Christ in another Old Testament book that, unlike Ruth, offers no pre-figuring of the New Testament—the *Song of Songs* or *Song of Solomon*. This is a book that appears lacking in any theological significance. Yet there it is, a part of sacred Scripture for centuries.

The language of the book relates the thoughts of two newlyweds. It is rather erotic in spots and is seldom read in public worship. Dr. Dennis Kinlaw, in his commentary on the book that is part of *The Wesleyan Bible Commentary* series, contends that the Song of Songs is a statement of the goodness and beauty of the sexual relationship within marriage. Given the fact that the erotic needs of humankind are among the greatest influences on behavior (especially male behavior), it is actually surprising that more such affirmation is not included in Scripture.

To digress a moment, men who are not familiar with the Song of Songs might be surprised at the wealth of material it provides that they can employ in romantic conversation with their significant other:

"Your hair is like a flock of goats streaming down Mt. Gilead."

"Your teeth are like a flock of ewes coming up fresh from the dipping."

"Your parted lips are like a pomegranate cut open."

But use these sparingly. They are potent!

Returning to the original point, even in this "non-theological" book from Paul's tradition, we can discover a metaphor for the powerful experience of love that drove the apostle from Jerusalem to Samaria to Judea to the uttermost parts of the world. What an awesome privilege he must have felt it to be as he encouraged the Philippian believers to reach for the same loving attitude toward others that Jesus' obedience so comprehensively illustrates.

Love: The Power to Transform

Do nothing out of selfish ambition or vain conceit, but in humility consider others better than yourselves. Each of you should look not only to your own interests, but also to the interests of others

Paul's experience is summed up in the title of a sermon by Thomas Chalmers, a Scotsman who lived in the 19th century. The title was "The Expulsive Power of a New Affection." In that message Chalmers endeavored to expose the power of love to transform a human life.

His basic thesis notes that negative forces, such as fear, are not nearly so healthy nor long lasting as those spawned by positive factors, such as the love of God. Put another way, you don't convince someone of the delights of springtime by griping about winter weather. In Jesus, God certainly reveals the springtime of his love for all people.

During the Welsh revival of the early twentieth century (1904), the expulsive power of love literally expelled stolen items from the homes of reawakened Christians. Over the years workers had pilfered all manner of things. When their lives were touched by the gracious love of God, they began returning these items. Large mounds of returned tools piled up, requiring several shipyards to put up signs that read: If You Have Been Led By God To Return What You Have Stolen, Please Know That The Management Forgives You And Wishes You To Keep What You Have Taken (quoted in *How to Be Pentecostal Without Speaking in Tongues*, A. Campolo, pp. 92-93).

The greatest influence upon the human heart is love. A "new affection," as Chalmers called it, can make the darkest day seem sunny. It can transport us to another world. When love strikes the heart it can expel most anything: hunger, fatigue, stinginess, hate. It can expel them with an ease that would be considered impossible if one were to set out deliberately to remove such thoughts.

It is not coincidental that in the list of the fruit of the Spirit found in Galatians 5, joy immediately follows love. They are both results of the work of God's Spirit. Both joy and love, as well as the rest of the other graces in the fruit of the Spirit, grow in the soil of faith. But this is not a generic faith. It is faith in the God and Father of our Lord Jesus Christ who is love. If it is not theologically imprecise to say it, the fruit of the Spirit listed from joy to self-control might be said to be fruits of love. God's love leads to joy, of that we may be sure. As he brings love into our hearts, it expels other attitudes and makes room for the rest of the fruit. A believer then sees opportunities for peace and patience and longsuffering through new eyes, eyes transformed by Christ's love.

Years ago an unusual house was built in New England to which a unique tower was attached. The owner used to take guests up into this tower to survey the surrounding countryside. At the top of the tower they would discover four glassed-in sides. Each side was a different color glass. One side was red, making the nearby hills appear hot and steamy. Another side was brown, giving the appearance of decay to the earth below. The next side was blue, leaving the visitor with a sense of wintry coolness. The remaining side was green, bathing the hillsides with the appearance of spring

(*Keeping Pace: Inspirations in the Air*, E. Fitzgerald, p. 200, Pace Communications). The love of God, first seen in Creation, observed in the characters of the old covenant, and brilliantly revealed in Jesus is not limited to optics, to a change in appearances. Praying for the Ephesian church, Paul asked that through Jesus Christ, God would open the eyes of their hearts (1:18). In today's terms, he did not seek a better pair of spiritual sunglasses. Writing here to the Philippians, he did not say, "for me to see things more comfortably is Christ." He spoke of organic, systemic change: "For me to live is Christ." This faith meant more than a superficial change. It went to the roots and transcended all of life.

> *Each of you should look not only to your own interests,*
> *but also to the interests of others.*

Craig Kenner, New Testament professor at Eastern Seminary in Philadelphia, tells of a prayer time he shared with a Nigerian seminarian named Sunday. Nigeria, like Sudan, has been a nation where violence has resulted in death and displacement for tens of thousands of Christians. As they prayed, word of the slaughter of women and children was fresh in their minds. Sunday's cousin had been killed, and there was a possibility his brothers, now missing, were also dead. Craig passionately prayed, "Rise up, O God! Avenge the blood of your servants!" Then Sunday opened his heart to the Lord, saying, "Please forgive the Muslims and spare them because they have no hope." Such a prayer does not come from spiritual contact lenses. It comes from the presence of God within, who can enable us literally to transcend, rise above our nature ("Mutual Mayhem," Craig Kenner, *Christianity Today*, Nov. '04, pp. 60-64, Vol. 48, No. 11).

In the summer of A.D. 386, Augustine, then thirty-two years old, sat weeping in the garden of his friend Alypius in Milan. He had been professor of rhetoric for two years in that city, a position that should have been satisfying. Such was not the case. He wanted to start a new life, but could not find the resolution to make a break with his past. As he sat, he heard a child singing in a neighboring house, *Tolle, lege! Tolle, lege!* ("Take up and read! Take up and read!) Taking up the scroll that lay at his friend's side—a copy of Paul's letters as it happened—he let his eye fall on what we know as the opening words of Romans 13: "not in reveling and drunkenness, not in debauchery and licentiousness, not in quarreling and jealousy; but put on the Lord Jesus Christ, and make no provision for the flesh, to gratify its desires." "No further would I read," he said, "nor had I any need; instantly, at the end of this sentence, a clear light flooded my heart and all the darkness of doubt vanished away" (quoted in *Paul: Apostle of the Heart Set Free*, F. F. Bruce, p. 470). The transcendent presence of Jesus Christ brought an inner resource the world could not give.

if any comfort from his love, if any fellowship with the Spirit

The famous chaplain G. Studdard Kennedy said that only passion can change passion. Augustine, a man of powerful passions, met a "new affection," a more powerful passion than his own. The love of Christ captured his heart as it had Paul's centuries earlier.

In the Song of Songs we hear newlyweds wax poetic about the power of love. As chapter two begins (vs. 4), the bride depicts the abundance of love which she feels, declaring, "He has taken me to the banquet hall, and his banner over me is love." Then she hears his invitation to arise and join him as he says, "See! The winter is past; the rains are over and gone. Flowers appear on the earth; the season of singing has come, the cooing of doves is heard in our land" (2:11-12). This Eastern-style, symbolic language was echoed in an expression used by a Palestinian tour guide I met in Israel. Always a showman, he spoke dramatically about his wife. Together they had brought a large family into the world as she had "taken him to the garden of high affection." Indeed, "high affection" is a powerful thing!

However, there is no affection, no love that compares to the love of God. Its power has been the wind beneath the wings of countless believers, from St. Paul to Mother Teresa to the multitude of anonymous Christians who have been compelled to stretch out their hands and seek God's kingdom, saying, "for me to *live* is Christ."

Naïvete—in The Eye of the Beholder

It should come as no surprise that the joy and hope that the powerful love of Christ has engendered in believers has been attacked as shallow and naive. Is it any more naive than the pessimism of the world? For example, a statesman once said, "Politicians have strained their ingenuity to discover new sources of revenue. They have broadened perilously the field of income and property tax. When I was a boy, wealth was regarded as secure and admirable, but now a man has to defend himself for being rich, as if it were a crime." That statesman was Socrates, who lived roughly 400 years before Jesus. He also said, "Our young people are rebelling against established authority. They are indifferent to convention and no longer neat in appearance. They are openly disobedient to their parents. If they are to become future leaders, there is indeed little hope for the world."

How about this, "They were long-haired, and young, and wore bright-colored clothing. Sometimes they frolicked in the streets nude, chanted obscenities at their elders—and consumed generous amounts of dope. Reared in an age of doomsday-oriented crises, they were protesting the growing, rampant materialism of their parents." That certainly has a contemporary ring to it. It was actually written in France in 1830.

In the late 18th century, British politician William Pitt declared, "There is scarcely anything around us but ruin and despair." In the following century, Prime Minister Benjamin Disraeli moaned, ". . . in industry, commerce and agriculture there is no hope."

This quote from a national magazine echoes Pitt's despair:

> It is a gloomy moment in history. Not in the lifetime of
> most people has there been such grave apprehension. Never
> has the future seemed so uncertain as this. In France, the
> political cauldron bubbles with uncertainty. Russia hangs,
> as usual, like a cloud, dark and silent upon the horizon of
> Europe. All the resources and energies of the British Empire
> are sorely tried . . . in coping with vast and deadly problems,
> and there are disturbed conditions in China. Of our own
> troubles in the United States, no man can see the end . . . The
> very haste to be rich is the occasion of much widespread
> calamity, and has tended to destroy moral forces (quoted in
> *You're in Charge*, Cecil Osborne, pp. 61-62).

This appeared in *Harper's* magazine well over 100 years ago.

Such quotes illustrate an obvious truth. Hopelessness and despair
are not necessarily signs of facing reality. They may just as easily
be indicators of a lack of vision or perspective. When we look at
life and see hopelessness, it is rather like looking in a mirror. You
see only one dimension. It is easy to miss what religious-myth
authority Joseph Campbell referred to as the believer's "invisible
means of support." The active love of God in which believers are
rooted often eludes the eye of the unbelieving beholder.

Believing is Seeing

Thinking that believing means seeing is one of the great dangers
of living in a visual age such as ours. We are constantly bombarded
with images, especially in the so-called "news." But we must never
think that what can be captured in a picture, even a moving picture,
tells the whole story. Beyond the "facts" and pictures there are other
dimensions, not the least of which is the dimension of faith. While
those who trust in Christ are sometimes accused of closing their
eyes to the harsh facts of life, the truth of the matter is that those

who do not believe fail to see all the dimensions of life. It isn't that believers do not see reality. They see more than the eye can capture, and as a result they find hope and joy, regardless of what appears to be.

If you have any encouragement from being united with Christ

Thomas Kelly, in his spiritual classic *A Testament of Devotion*, written during World War II, observes this reality through the eyes of faith, writing,

> Out in front of us is the drama of men and nations, seething, struggling, laboring, dying. Upon this tragic drama in these days our eyes are all set in anxious watchfulness and in prayer. But within the silences of the souls of men an eternal drama is ever being enacted, in these days as well as in others. And on the outcome of this inner drama rests, ultimately, the outer pageant of history. It is the drama of the Hound of Heaven baying relentlessly upon the track of man. It is the drama of the lost sheep wandering in the wilderness, restless and lonely, feebly searching, while over the hills comes the wiser Shepherd. For His is a shepherd's heart, and He is restless until He holds His sheep in His arms. It is the drama of the Eternal Father drawing the prodigal home unto Himself, where there is bread enough and to spare. It is the drama of the Double Search, as Rufus Jones calls it. And always its chief actor is—the Eternal God of Love (p. 51).

Faith in and of itself is a powerful force. Faith that unbelievers have in science, for example, has lead to remarkable achievements. And while it has its limits, there is power in positive thinking (just as there is great power in negative thinking). When faith is focused on a worthy object, its power is exponentially multiplied. For Christians that object is God revealed in the Old Testament and in Jesus Christ, who did "nothing out of selfish ambition or vain conceit" (2:3). This object is not just the Creator who hung the planets in space. This Creator also hung on a cross. This Creator not only commands us to love him, but loves us beyond our ability to imagine it. For Christians God rules a dimension of life that cynics and naysayers do not see when they examine their daily existence.

Aleksandr Solzhenitsyn, Russian dissident and author, lived through the horrors of political oppression in Communist Russia. His book *The Gulag Archipelago* relates the inhumanities imposed upon people during this time. Yet he is a person of hope, a man committed to Christ. As a result of the cross, he believes there is a power at work that nothing can ultimately kill. Having seen what happens to a society, where the leadership rejects the spiritual dimension of faith, he more fully appreciates the power of the unseen.

make my joy complete by being like-minded,
having the same love, being one in spirit and in purpose

Author Philip Yancey tells the story of this unseen power of God influencing people in East Germany in the final years before the Berlin Wall fell. Beginning in 1982, four churches in Leipzig held weekly prayer meetings every Monday evening at 5:00. At first a handful of Christians gathered. In time the crowds began to swell, attracting not just faithful Christians but also political dissidents and ordinary citizens. The church was the one place where the Communist state allowed freedom of assembly. After these meetings the groups would join together and walk through the dark streets of Leipzig, holding candles and banners in simple protest. Virtually every demonstration in the country began in such a fashion, in worship.

In time the Western media picked up the story and oppression began. Secret police surrounded the churches, sometimes roughing up the marchers. Still the crowds grew, up to 50,000. On October

9, 1989, a sense of impending crisis was palpable. East German leader Erich Honecker gave orders to shoot the demonstrators. It looked like another Tiananmen Square in the making.

No one knows for sure why, but that night as 70,000 protestors marched, no shots were fired. The following Monday 120,000 marched. A week later, 500,000 turned out—nearly the entire population of Leipzig.

In early November almost one million people marched peacefully through East Berlin. Erich Honecker resigned in humiliation. At midnight on November 9 the unexpected became history: a gap opened up in the Berlin Wall.

As Bud Bultman, a producer and writer for CNN, later wrote,

> We in the media watched in astonishment as the walls of totalitarianism came crashing down. But in the rush to cover the cataclysmic events, the story behind the story was overlooked. We trained our cameras on hundreds of thousands of people praying for freedom, votive candles in hand, and yet we missed the transcendent dimension, the explicitly spiritual and religious character of the story. We looked right at it and could not see it.

Several weeks after the October 9 turning point, a huge banner appeared across a Leipzig street: *Wir danken Dir, Kirche* (We thank you, church), (Philip Yancey, *Finding God in Unexpected Places*, pp. 133-36).

But this was not the case with the apostle Paul. He saw beyond what a camera might capture. On the "film" of his heart there appeared an image, the image of God revealed in Jesus, an image of compelling love. As Paul's life "developed," that image became more and more apparent to those who knew him. In writing to this young congregation at Philippi, a brilliant hue appeared in the picture, the vibrant shade of joy developing in the chemistry of agape.

To this day, all who stretch out their hands to the Lord and "expose" their hearts to this light, discover that same image of love. As they walk in that light, the deep shades of joy begin to appear, evidence of the delight of the love of Jesus.

The early verses of Philippians 2 remind me of the comments of the English lay theologian G. K. Chesterton with regard to the Sermon on the Mount. He observed that the first time you read it, it seems to turn everything upside down. But then you realize, in its high calling, it actually turns everything right side up. Surely the same is true of the love we must receive by grace in order to live in the kind of healing humility of which Paul writes.

I find myself resonating with the words of a man who could not see with his physical eyes, but whose "heart-sight" was 20/20. The blind poet and pastor George Matheson saw the answer to our need and wrote this prayer:

> O love that wilt not let me go,
> I rest my weary soul in Thee.
> I give Thee back the life I owe,
> That in Thine ocean depths its flow
> May richer, fuller be.

As we move to the holy ground of Philippians 2:5-11, we sense the joy for which this epistle is known, the joy of the Lord, the joy of abiding in the kind of Savior Paul will remind us Jesus is.

Questions for Discussion

1. When is it productive to compare ourselves to others? When is it counter-productive?
2. What did Becky Pippert mean when she said, "Only what transcends us can transform us."? Can you think of examples of this truth?

3. How do you picture God? What is he like? Why does it matter to you?

4. What difference would it make to you if you believed that the heart of God beats for you with love of the deepest kind?

5. Has love ever expelled something from your life?

6. The "high affection" of sexual intimacy is a gift from God. Why did God give such a gift?

7. Is pessimism more realistic than optimism? Why?

8. Why does focused positive or negative thinking have power?

9. How much support for faith should we expect from the secular world? From the media? From government?

10. Why does Jesus "turn things right side up"?

CHAPTER SEVEN

Break a Vase—Reaching Beyond Your Mind to His

Philippians 2:5-11

Your attitude should be the same as that of Christ Jesus: Who being in very nature God, did not consider equality with God something to be grasped, but made himself nothing, taking the very nature of a servant, being made in human likeness. And being found in appearance as a man, he humbled himself and became obedient to death—even death on a cross! Therefore God exalted him to the highest place and gave him the name that is above every name, that at the name of Jesus every knee should bow, in heaven and on earth and under the earth, and every tongue confess that Jesus Christ is Lord, to the glory of God the Father.

The birth of our first child was a fast ride on a sharp learning curve. My wife and I, both college graduates, assumed we knew as much as we needed to know about "birthin' babies." Well, experiences like that first childbirth have led me to a fundamental assumption: Most assumptions are wrong.

As humbling as the reality of childbirth proved to be, when the agony of labor was over, the ecstasy of being parents seemed to absolve us of our ignorance. I still vividly recall being directed by a nurse to a large glass window, where for the first time I saw my little girl. The earth . . . no . . . the universe moved under my feet. Cosmic awe flooded my entire being from the follicles to the feet.

It was something similar to the experience of a fellow college student who had encountered the presence of God in an unusual revival service. Feeling the poverty of any words to describe the wonder of the moment, he declared, "It was such a holy place that when you came forward to the altar you just wanted to…take your feet off!"

Such are my spiritual sensibilities when I read Philippians 2:5-11. The information we encounter in this passage should shake our lives to the core. It is impossible to exaggerate the significance of what Paul affirms. Here it is revealed to us that Jesus Christ:

> did not cling to his equality with God,
> made himself nothing,
> took the form of a servant,
> was obedient unto death—on a cross,
> has been exalted to the highest place,
> will one day be worshiped by all.

These declarations were not based on theories. What is lifted up in praise occurred in time and space, in flesh and blood. This is an awestruck witness to quintessential humility, obedience and love.

Maybe you've heard about the rabbi who went into the temple to pray. As he knelt, another rabbi praying nearby cried out, "I am nothing! Nothing!" The listening rabbi muttered in a stage whisper, "Look who thinks he's nothing!"

Jesus' humility was not revealed in pious exclamations uttered in the warm glow of stained-glass windows. God did not send a message. God sent a Messenger. To paraphrase Marshall McCluhan, philosopher of the world of modern media, the Messenger was the message.

Therefore God exalted him to the highest place and gave him a name above every name, that at the name of Jesus every knee should bow, in heaven and on earth and under the earth, and every tongue confess that Jesus Christ is Lord, to the glory of God the Father.

Paul, who never feared overstatement when praising Jesus, literally sings out in prophetic certainty that one day every knee will bow to Jesus and every tongue will confess his lordship to the glory of God the Father.

The awe generated by the humble service of someone like Mother Teresa, which compelled even the secular world to bow in amazed recognition, will be multiplied over and over in worship of the Lamb. God's wondrous love revealed in the obedience of Jesus will generate a mighty gravitational pull, compelling every knee to bow.

A Call to Extravagant Employment

As magnificent as the content of this scripture is, its claims might remain in the realm of poetry were it not for the brief proclamation that precedes it in verse five, "Your attitude should be the same as that of Christ Jesus," or the familiar words of the King James version, "Let this mind be in you, which was also in Christ Jesus." These words are not a call for summer soldiers and sunshine patriots. This is an invitation to employment—to vocation—accompanied by a daunting job description.

Yet there is something absolutely blessed about this call to humility. What would life be apart from the import of Philippians 2:5-11? Victor Hugo said that without dreams life is like a broken-winged bird that cannot fly. Without this call to the victorious surrender of those who follow Jesus Christ, life would be a broken-winged bird, looking longingly into the skies for which it was made, but forever shackled to the earth. Apart from emptying ourselves of any desire to be like God, apart from service, apart from obedience to truth, apart from a spiritual second childhood, human potential is hollow. Apart from the hope that taking up the cross in obedient faithfulness will lead to resurrections, life is a cynical cycle of despair that slams us into the earth from which we are only a highly evolved life-form.

Without Philippians 2:5-11 in the lexicon of human history, Jesus is a luxury that mocks our sin-bound lives.

Thankfully, these words are ours to apprehend and by which to be apprehended.

Just as the humility of Jesus brings us to our knees in awe, so the possibilities of having his mind and his attitude in us pulls our spirits upward. The unique power and authority that marks the Bible as God's Word can be felt by receiving this high calling. Allow me, then, to step aside for a moment and let God speak to you: Let your attitude be the same as that of Christ Jesus. (Yes, I mean you!)

An intriguing example of this is found in Mark 14. In an act of extravagant love, Jesus is anointed by a woman who breaks open a vase filled with perfume valued at a year's wages. In response to this deed, Jesus states, ". . . wherever the gospel is preached in the whole world, that which this woman has done shall be spoken in memory of her" (14:9). Why? Because "she had that mind which was in Christ Jesus" when she did it.

As a result of this verse, Chuck Swindoll, noting how actors tell each other to "Break a leg!" suggests that Christians should exhort one another by saying "Break a vase!"

Be extravagant! Let Christ be poured out through your continuously surrendered will.

Wouldn't it be fantastic if on judgment day an agent of the FBI (Forever Bureau of Investigation) would step forward as you are judged and say, "Your Honor, I want to report on the crime scene (earth). We have in our file a record of having found this person's fingerprints on needy lives. Prints have been lifted off broken hearts and lives both young and old alike. The pages of this suspect's Bible are covered with fingerprints. Several persons who harmed this person show evidence of having been unreasonably forgiven. On the basis of this and similar evidence, we hereby charge this person with having the mind that was in Christ Jesus!"

Break a vase!

Humility: Not Normal but Not Unnatural

he humbled himself and became obedient to death

In this context it seems to be exactly what we ought to do. The only problem is that we don't usually live with such a picture in our minds. Talk of breaking vases is painful. It smacks of taking up one's cross, of humility and obedience—the kind that requires suffering. As Simon Peter, such a suggestion prompts us to take Jesus aside for a rebuke, a rejection of the cross.

> He [Jesus] spoke plainly about this [the cross], and Peter took him aside and began to rebuke him. But when Jesus turned and looked at his disciples, he rebuked Peter. "Get behind me, Satan!" He said. "You do not have in mind the things of God, but the things of men" (Mark 8:32-33).

Vases of the world, take heart! You have a friend in Satan.

For years I failed really to hear Jesus speaking through this portion of Philippians because the image of self-emptying of which it speaks struck me as an aberration. God loved the world so much that God went outside the box and gave his Son, or so I generally thought. But that was not clear thinking. While the Incarnation was unique, nothing is abnormal about God's having a self-emptying heart. It is part of God's nature. This is the way God thinks. In a word, this is love. That was a moving realization. But the real impact of such truth was yet to dawn.

taking the very nature of a servant, being made in human likeness

From this insight comes one even more remarkable. It is also part of human nature as created by God to be self-emptying. We are made in God's image. When Rick Warren in *The Purpose-Driven Life* lists one of humankind's purposes as being "shaped to serve," he is right on target.

There is no more commonly prayed prayer, though usually subconscious, than "let this cup pass from me." We cling to ourselves and want our cups to stay as full as possible. But that does not mean we were designed that way. Jesus dramatically lived out both his deity and his humanity in accepting that cup. He was shaped to serve, to accept the "cup" of self-giving, and so are we!

Jesus, the second Adam, was God's re-start of human creation. Faithful in the way the nation of Israel was supposed to have been, in the way humankind was supposed to have been, Jesus was the old covenant incarnate. Author and professor Richard Foster in his powerful book *Freedom of Simplicity*, writes of the prophet Jeremiah filing a "malpractice suit" against the people of the old covenant. Philippians 2:5-11 is God's fresh call through Jesus Christ to be what God's people were supposed to be all along. In truth that malpractice suit could have been filed against every human life from the beginning. Think of it. What if Adam and Eve had "emptied themselves" of their perceived rights to exercise God-like judgment? Their experience portends human history, a history which the New Testament affirms, in the wake of Jesus Christ, need no longer be hopelessly repeated by reborn children of God.

Shine, Jesus, Shine

In the section of scripture that follows, Paul refers to Christians who shine like stars (2:15). The image is that of a bright light against a dark background. This invitation to have the mind of Christ is our invitation to plug into the "star power" of him who is the Light of the world. In the Sermon on the Mount in Matthew 5:14-16, Jesus says, "You are the light of the world. A city on a hill cannot be hidden. Neither do people light a lamp and put it under a bowl. Instead they put it on its stand, and it gives light to everyone in the house. In the same way, let your light shine before men, that they may see your good deeds and praise your Father in heaven."

How do we become filaments aglow with his light? We break the vase (or bowl, as Jesus said) of pride and allow the oxygen of God's Spirit to ignite the flame of faith within us "to the glory of God the Father" (2:11).We chose not to "consider equality with God something to be grasped" (2:6).

To borrow an illustration from astronomy, we give up our desire to be the sun and take our proper place as a moon. The sun, the center of the universe, generates its own light. A moon does not generate its own light, but reflects the light of the sun. Jesus, as God, was at the center of everything, but showed us our proper place by taking the place of a servant, a "moon," and allowing the Father fully to reflect himself.

In so doing he revealed the spiritual irony that breaking the vase of pride opens the floodgates that release rivers of living water (John 7:38). We are called, with hands outstretched like children toward a loving Father, to empty ourselves of lesser things and to grasp above for grace. The heartbeat of joy for which this letter is known finds its pulse right here.

Being Found: Reflecting Our Citizenship

he humbled himself and became obedient

In Luke 19:10, at the conclusion of Jesus' encounter with Zacheaus, Jesus declares, "The Son of Man has come to seek and to save the lost." What does it mean to be lost? It means not knowing where you are. The humility referred to in this passage grows out of a clear understanding of where we are: We are in God's creation. We are intended to glorify the Creator and to love and obey him above all else. To lose this perspective is to be lost.

The mind that was in Christ Jesus is a way of thinking that knows who we are and where we are. The pride that obscures this relationship must be broken. We must accept our role, not as the source of life, but as reflectors of the true source of life and light.

In Philippians 1:27 we are told to conduct ourselves in a manner worthy of the gospel of Christ. This is a reminder to believers who "know where we are," citizens of the eternal world, what Jesus referred to as the kingdom of God. The kingdom of God is that network of spiritual relationships wherein the citizens live in an awareness of who they are and to whom they belong. The word "conduct" has a Greek root associated with the word politics. The idea, then, is this: behave like good citizens of the kingdom of God.

Consider a sign that was seen on the side of a truck owned by a scuba-diving business. The message was simple: "One earth—two worlds." While the sign referred to both the world above and below the surface of the water, we as Christians also ought to be aware that there are two worlds. There is a world that can be seen with the physical eye and a world that can be seen only with what Paul called in Ephesians 1:18, "the eyes of your heart." As those eyes are enlightened, we know ourselves to be "found" by him who came to seek and to save. When we meet him, our journey toward humility begins.

In Philippians 1:27 and following, the church is spoken of as a sign to the lost world. Then from 2:15 on, Paul speaks of Christians as shining like stars in a dark world. In between is the magnificent call to seek the humility of Jesus. The sum total of these verses is a call for the church to bear witness to the unseen world of the kingdom. In his book *A Shattered Visage*, Ravi Zacharias tells of an experience that mirrors this role.

> While traveling to Chicago by train, I sat behind a man and his young son. The boy seemed intrigued by the passing scenery and described to his father everything that he saw. He talked about some children at play in a schoolyard. He mentioned the rocks in a small stream and described the sunlight's reflection on the water. When we stopped for a freight train to cross our track, the boy tried to guess what each car might be hauling. As we neared the city he expressed excitement over the waves of Lake Michigan and told about the many boats in dry dock. At the end of the trip I leaned forward and said to the father, "How refreshing to enjoy the world through the eyes of a child!" He smiled and replied,

"Yes, it is. Especially if it's the only way you can see it." He was blind (p. 130).

When we share a Christ-like attitude, we reflect this love to others, illuminating God's kingdom and exposing it to the blind world. We sometimes refer to this as "witnessing." When Christians assume this servant attitude, the world cannot help but witness his nature.

A husband comes into my office. He is the strong, silent type. It looks as if the weight of the world is on his shoulders. Slowly he unfolds the story of his wife's unfaithfulness. When it comes time to leave he looks at me and says, "I would forgive her without hesitation and take her back." He thinks as God thinks, a pattern of divine reasoning revealed in the thoughts of Jesus.

One of the poorest senior citizens of the church telephones and says she must see me. With some consternation I go. After my arrival I learn that she has come into a windfall of $15,000 and wants to give me a check for 10% of it for the work of Christ through the church. Jesus has appeared again among "the least of these."

We take a van full of folks to a special event. One of the travelers is a woman who is mentally challenged. As the person in charge, I am a bit anxious because I must help her into her seat. Everyone includes her in the conversation and treats her with unassuming kindness. As the trip later concludes, it is clear to me that both she and I have been ministered to by the presence of the Lord.

All of these situations begin with a "break a vase" attitude where pride is concerned.

Faith's Opportunity to Shine: The Person Right in Front of Us

The first four verses of Philippians 2 make it clear that adopting a Christ-like attitude is not a mental exercise. We are not simply meant to fill our hard drive with Jesus stuff. No, that would be a 180° misunderstanding of what Paul is saying.

The mind of Christ is always concrete. It is never to be understood abstractly. Christianity is always incarnational. In following the mind of Christ, as noted in the last chapter, we in the church are told:

> be like minded,
> have the same love,
> be one in spirit and in purpose,
> do nothing out of ambition or conceit,
> consider others before ourselves,
> look not only to our own interests, but also
> the interests of others.

Anyone can love "people" as a whole. The encouragement we experience from being united with Christ, the comfort of his love, our fellowship with his Spirit (2:1) are all intended to help us love the *person* in front of us, not just people in general. The "mind of Christ" is an attitude that looks people in the eye.

Economist E. F. Schumaker, a young statistician during World War I, worked on a farm. Each day he counted the 32 head of cattle for which he was responsible, and then went on to something else. One day an old farmer told him that if he only *counted* the cattle, they would not flourish. Sure enough, one day he counted only 31 head of cattle; one was dead in the bushes. He finally understood the old farmer's advice. It was more important to know the condition of each animal than to know how many he had (Sally Cunneen, *The Christian Century*, quoted in *Leadership*, Summer 1986, Vol. VII, Number 3, p. 38).

As followers of the Good Shepherd, we follow an example that requires us to care for persons one at a time. Love does that. Divine love knows that we are relational creatures and this is how we experience love.

One of the top-selling books of all time is Dr. Benjamin Spock's *Baby and Child Care*, with 40 million copies in print. In one of his latter books, Dr. Spock wrote of his concern that the world is not a better place than it was in 1903 when he was born. He believed that it is due to people not investing in relationships. We are more interested in our standard of living than the quality of the bonds between us. He blames this for the moral and cultural decline in our country.

We ought not to be surprised. The "mind of Adam" is an attitude that discourages relationships. Why? Because it is centered in a desire for control.

Want to Be Like God? Be Broken.

did not consider equality with God something to be grasped

It is incredibly ironic. From the genesis of human experience people have had the wrong picture of God. God is control, so they thought. And they want to be like God. But the projection of their own desire onto God leads them into pain and sorrow.

Christians cannot be content to judge the unbelieving world and leave themselves unexamined. Paul had just such a self-examination in mind when he wrote 1 Corinthians. 1 Corinthians 13:1-3 is, for me, one of the most challenging portions of the Bible. In these verses, spiritually alive, gifted, apparently compassionate and self-sacrificing Christians are called to task. Such persons are fully capable, it is announced, of being the captives of control even in the company of spiritual power, spiritual experiences and gifts. Televangelists like Jim Baker and Jimmy Swaggart expose the possibility of gifted people making themselves ends instead of means in God's kingdom. As a pastor of more than 30 years, now moving beyond middle age, I can testify that these highly visible examples are not alone in missing God's mark. I look back with surprise and disappointment at some of the self-glorifying motives that propelled my hard work for the Lord.

We can speak in tongues, have the gifts of prophecy and

understand mysteries, move mountains with our faith, give away all that we have and end our lives as martyrs, and still miss the point. A desire to be more like the sun than a moon, even if apparently spiritual and compassionate in its expression, is still contrary to the mind of Christ.

This is a call to a complete, vase-breaking surrender to God.

Scott Peck in *The Road Less Traveled and Beyond* reflects on his earlier observation in *The Road Less Traveled* when he said that human beings are to evolve toward the point of becoming like God. This suggestion, he recalls, created a great deal of "spiritual indigestion." He goes on to say, "I could have prevented much of this indigestion had I gone on to write about the great paradox involved. The paradox is that we ourselves cannot become like God except by bumping ourselves off, except through the humility of emptiness" (p. 270).

C. S. Lewis states this in words remarkable for their spiritual and psychological depth:

> It is no good trying to be myself without Him. The more I resist Him and try to live on my own, the more I become dominated by my own heredity and upbringing and natural desires. In fact, what I so proudly call 'myself' becomes merely the meeting place for trains of events which I never started and which I cannot stop. What I call 'my wishes' becomes merely the desires thrown up by my physical organism or pumped into me by other men's thoughts or even suggested to me by devils . . . most of what I call me can be very easily explained. It is when I turn to Christ, when I give myself up to His personality, that I begin to have a real personality of my own (*Mere Christianity*, 187).

When Jesus told Nicodemus that he needed a new birth, was not this what he meant: a *new mind*? What is the source of that mind? "I have been crucified with Christ and I no longer live, but Christ lives in me" (Galatians 2:20). "The mind of sinful man is death, but the mind controlled by the Spirit is life and peace" (Romans 8:6). "Do not conform any longer to the pattern of this world, but be transformed by the renewing of your mind. Then you will be able to test and approve what God's will is—his good, pleasing and perfect will" (Romans 12:2).

Our choice is whether to possess the "mind of Adam" or the "mind of Christ." Do we expect the world to rotate around us, or around the risen Lord?

Anne Ortland shares her husband's sermon on the story of Mary breaking the vase of expensive perfume and anointing Jesus. She was surprised to hear that when the vase was broken, the whole house was full of its fragrance.

By contrast she observed how often Christians come into church on Sunday morning like alabaster vases—contained, self-sufficient, no sweet scent coming from us. The outside looks fine, maybe even beautiful.

Perhaps that picture makes it clear how shocking it was for Mary to break her vase. After all, this had not been a vase-breaking party. Anne concludes that people file into church week after week because Jesus is in them, but so often they do not let him out. She writes, "The need for Christians everywhere (nobody is exempt) is to be broken. The vase has to be smashed. Christians have to let the life out. It will fill the room with sweetness. And the congregation will all be broken shards, mingling together for the first time" (quoted in *Living Above the Level of Mediocrity*, C. Swindoll, 72-73).

What a picture! Take in the heavenly odor of a congregation full of broken vases!

Imagine going to see a surgeon, concerned that you have a serious problem. You have not felt good. Weariness has been your constant companion. The doctor examines you and says, "I've got good news. Your problem is due to the fact that Jesus is bottled up inside you and needs to be let out."

Today I had a lengthy discussion with our youth pastor about his plans for the months ahead. He commented on his frustration that so much effort and expense goes into evangelism events. It isn't that he opposes evangelism. It is his sense that these events focus so intently on the individual, getting Jesus into the hearts, the vases, of young lives. He went on to say, it can be really hard to help new believers understand that a major reason for getting Jesus into us is in order then to let him back out!

Out of my vast theological wisdom, I tried to comfort him with the thought that the process of entering into justification by faith was a selfish process. We are driven by deep needs. However, in the process of sanctification, we are allowing God to conform our needs to his. The Holy Spirit calls us to break a vase and let Jesus out. When this happens the mind of Christ is at work. Jesus said, in so many words, "those who protect the Savior will end up empty." "Those who break the vase and let him out, will be full."

By faith we invite Jesus into our vase to cleanse and fill it. So far so good. It is a fine thing to care for our vase, to polish it and keep it filled with faith. However, the true beauty of this vase is not seen until it is cracked by love seeking a way out. That kind of love is the manifestation of the mind of Christ.

and every tongue confess that Jesus Christ is Lord
to the glory of God the Father

Dr. W. L Hitchcock, one of the members of a congregation I served, died unexpectedly. Dr. Hitchcock was a highly respected and revered professor in guidance counseling. His peers and students alike were of one voice in ranking him as a superior person and professional. I did not know him in that part of his life. By the time I met Dr. Hitchcock he was involved in a different career: full-time care giver for his wife who was the victim of Alzheimer's disease.

Dr. Hitchcock was a highly decorated veteran of World War II. His right leg was stiff from the hip down due to an encounter with enemy fire. When Mrs. Hitchcock grew too much for his aging body to care for, she entered a nursing home. Almost any day when

I walked by her room I saw Dr. Hitchcock sitting by her bedside, his slanted posture readily identifying his presence.

Over and over again I detected the glory of God present and the mind of Christ at work as the perfume of serving love filled the room.

In the concluding remarks at his funeral service, I told what I had learned only the day before. At Dr. Hitchcock's retirement ceremony, he had made this statement, "The most important decision I ever made was to accept Jesus Christ as my Savior and Lord." In my final sentence I remarked, "We greatly appreciate your telling us that, Hitch, but the truth is, we knew. We knew."

To be sure, that decision was indeed of the utmost significance. It set a foundation for what followed. But in light of Philippians 2:5-11, I would add, "Dr. Hitchcock, I rejoice that you decided to let Jesus in. But I am even more thankful that you let Jesus out."

Mrs. Hitchcock was unaware that her husband had died. But in the mystery of love, two weeks after his death she joined him in eternity. What an awesome thing it is when two persons become one, especially when the other person is Jesus.

Questions for Discussion

1. Jesus is referred to elsewhere in Paul's writings as the second Adam. Compare and contrast the first and second Adam. Which are we more like?

2. What has God done in Jesus to help us be like the second Adam—Jesus?

3. For whom are you or have you been willing to "break a vase"? Why? What does your motivation say about the true nature of holiness/sanctification/Christian perfection/the mind of Christ?

4. If we are designed to serve, what keeps us from doing it? What releases us to fulfill this aspect of God's image in us?

5. In chapter eight of *Mere Christianity* C.S. Lewis writes of pride as "the great sin." What qualities of pride might earn this common human characteristic that title?

6. What kind of behavior do you associate with spiritual lostness? How might this be related to numbness about living in the loving Father's creation?

7. You may have heard the admonition, "Witness at all times. Use words if necessary." What is the place of deeds and the place of words in witnessing to our faith?

8. The famous existentialist John Paul Sartre once said, "Hell is other people." What do you think he meant? How do we rise above such an attitude?

9. Suicide bombers literally give their bodies to be burned. Paul describes this extreme but still mis-motivated sacrifice in 1 Corinthians 13. Do they have the mind of Christ in their extreme self-giving? How do they illustrate Paul's concern in 1 Corinthians 13:1-3?

10. How do we bottle Jesus up inside us? What can enable us to let him out?

CHAPTER EIGHT

Holding onto Joy: Reaching Out for the God Who Is Great and Good

Philippians. 2:12-18

. . . my dear friends, as you have always obeyed—not only in my presence, but now much more in my absence—continue to work out your salvation with fear and trembling, for it is God who works in you to will and to act according to his good purpose Do everything without complaining or arguing, so that you may become blameless and pure, children of God without fault in a crooked and depraved generation, in which you shine like stars in the universe as you hold out the word of life—in order that I may boast on the day of Christ that I did not run or labor for nothing. But even if I am being poured out like a drink offering on the sacrifice and service coming from your faith, I am glad and rejoice with all of you. So you too should be glad and rejoice with me.

Joy...
One of the blessings of the fruit of the Holy Spirit is the joy which can be a distinguishing sign of the presence of God in one's life. A rephrased old saying asks, "If you were arrested for being a Christian, would there be enough joy to convict you?"

C. H. Dodd, widely respected New Testament scholar of the mid-twentieth century, noted that in the book of Acts wherever the young Christian church went it left a trail of joy. This observation has served as both a challenge and as a rebuke to me.

Do I leave a trail of joy wherever I go?

Can the people I serve be accused of joyful spiritual littering?

One of the most consequential Christian conversions of modern times was that of C. S. Lewis. Reluctantly embracing the Christian faith after a life of unbelief, Lewis wrote a narrative of his journey to Christian faith. He didn't name it *Surprised by Logic* or *Surprised by Guilt*. Neither did he name it *Surprised by the High Cost of Being a Christian*. He entitled it *Surprised by Joy*. Is it really unexpected that Lewis found joy so surprising? Will everyone who thinks of joy when you think of church hold up your hand. That's what I thought.

We would certainly not expect a non-believer to link these two together. To those who think as the world thinks, biblical faith equals *thou shalt not* (or to paraphrase the bumper sticker, Know Christ—No! No!). Are believers all that different? We hear the call, "Take up your cross and follow me" (what Philip Yancey called "the least manipulative invitation ever given"), and Christian joy becomes an oxymoron by default (*The Jesus I Never Knew*, p. 80).

When Commitment Sunday for the annual budget campaign arrives, how many people do cartwheels down the aisle, rejoicing in the opportunity to "give away" money? Does a fist fight break out between church members over who will teach the seventh-grade Sunday school class? In spite of talk about the "joy of Jesus," there is a dissonance within us that reflects a natural hesitance to associate joy with a life of obedience.

Not So Great Expectations

Why is joy exceptional? Some would suggest it is because people need a deeper surrender to God. Others would conclude that joyless people need to be "filled with the Holy Spirit." Still others would suggest a need for counseling or perhaps point to the influence of genetics. There is truth in all of these.

While I do not presume to know the answer, it seems certain that at the roots of joy is the soil of our view of God (as discussed in chapter 6). These words, Philipians 2:12-13, go to the heart of the matter: "Therefore, my dear friends, as you have always obeyed—not only in my presence, but now much more in my absence—

continue to work out your salvation with fear and trembling, for it is God who works in you to will and to act according to his good purpose." Paul is clearly pointing to a specific kind of God.

Years ago our denomination welcomed a new bishop by holding regional worship services. His sermon stuck in my mind, though at the time I was not impressed with its depth. The two points of his message were these: God is great; God is good. My attitude regarding that sermon is akin to Mark Twain's adolescent attitude toward his father. When he was 18 his father seemed like a fool. But by the time he turned 21, he was amazed at how much his father had learned. The same is true for me. The bishop's remarks have undergone a similar transformation. Juxtaposing God's greatness and God's goodness is a necessary exercise if joy is to grow in our lives.

David Seamands noted that J. B. Phillips' book *Your God Is Too Small* was a needed antidote for those whose view of God lacked wonder and awe. Dr. Seamands went on to say that a sequel is desperately needed to address those with distorted views of God's goodness: *Your God Is Too Mean.*

If we were to read Philippians 2:12-13 apart from what has been revealed to us about God in Jesus Christ, it might appear that God is a control freak. It all depends on how we perceive God's "good pleasure." The question is, is God's good pleasure good for us?

In Jesus, God revealed a remarkable balance between control and vulnerability. The control that God exercises is that of a servant. As Jesus calls us to take up our cross and follow him, he is calling us to balance our human desire for control with the "not-in- control" spirit of a servant. What does this have to do with joy?

Sometimes Joy Hides

Ultimate joy is the fruit of being controlled solely by God and no one else. Joy is the fruit of being a servant of the powerful God of creation who works in us for his good purpose. Joy is the fruit of knowing that fear and trembling is part of being human, part of living before God and part of escaping from the cocoon of a controlling kind of perfectionism. It is the born-again simplicity of a child that is at rest in his father's love.

for it is God who works in you

Joy is the fruit of an ongoing relationship with this God. What an amazing and wonderful thing it is to believe that *God works in you to will and to act according to his good purpose.* To experience joy is to live with an awareness that God is always the Senior Partner of those who believe, the *good* Senior Partner. The path to joy always and inevitably leads to this fact.

When church members ask their pastor to meet them at the doctor's office, the expectations are seldom hopeful. Such a visit is fresh in my mind as I write these words. I met them at the doctor's office because of what my parishioners expected to be told—pancreatic cancer. While I was there to support them, it was I who was blessed as they tearfully affirmed their faith in God to supervise the ultimate outcome of this most unwelcome turn of events. Did I experience joy? If you equate joy with happiness, I was about a million miles from it. Yet, beneath us as we wept were the everlasting arms of the Lord. Joy was there, but in respect for the pain, it was silently waiting for another time to be revealed. As we flew half-way across the country for the funeral, joy began to greet us who mourned, like a child playing hide-and-seek and clearing his throat to give away his hidden presence. We said our formal good-byes to a beloved husband and precious friend with humble confidence that, in spite of our sorrow, nothing had separated us from the love of God (or more importantly, the God of love).

When a new pastor begins ministering in a congregation, a period of months passes before he/she becomes aware of the pain to which he/she preaches every Sunday. But you know it is there. You know a big part of your calling is the challenge to help "your people" to be surprised by the joy of knowing God who was in

Christ, reconciling the pain of the world unto himself. Philippians was written for such a purpose. It is the epistle of joy because it is a witness to the God whose good pleasure was expressed in humble love.

Ray Steadman, the great Bible teacher, wrote,

> Remember, though, do not try to start with peace. When you get troubled or upset, when attacks come, do not try to start with making your heart feel at peace. This is a mistake many people make. They try to conjure up some kind of feeling of peace within and succeed only in upsetting themselves more. Do not start with peace. Start with truth. Work your way back down through truth and righteousness and you will come out at peace (*Spiritual Warfare*, p. 87).

What do you do when you lose your joy? Maybe you start talking to yourself, telling yourself to get a grip, telling yourself to calm down, to cheer up. Ray Steadman is right. That is not the place to begin. The place to start is to recognize the truth that you are in the hands of God. He is our peace. His *purpose* is always good. Circumstances can blind us to this. Faith is the lens through which we continue to see God as he is, regardless of circumstances. Only in faith can joy regularly be found.

even if I am being poured out like a drink offering . . . I am glad and rejoice with all of you. So you too should be glad and rejoice with me

Friend or Foe?

Several years ago an Eastern newspaper reported the following story. One evening a woman was coming home when she noticed a huge truck behind her that was driving uncomfortably close. She stepped on the gas to gain some distance, but when she sped up, the truck did too. The faster she drove, the faster the truck came on.

Now scared, she exited the freeway. But the truck stayed with her.

The woman then turned up a main street, hoping to lose her pursuer in traffic, but the truck ran a red light and continued the chase.

Reaching a point of panic, the woman whipped her car into a service station and bolted out the door screaming for help. The truck driver sprang from his truck and ran toward the car. Yanking the back door open, the driver pulled out a man hidden in the back seat.

She had been running from the wrong person. From his high vantage point, the truck driver had somehow realized that there was a would-be attacker in the woman's car. The chase was not his effort to harm her, but to save her (*Leadership*, 1986, Vol. VII, No. 3, p. 39).

So much depends on what we believe God's motives to be. If we believe he is good, then we are ready to rest in the Lord and experience joy. If we do not believe God's purposes are good, joy will always elude us.

I led a Sunday school class that included a very bright young woman from a strict family. One Sunday the subject was Psalm 139, which affirms the omnipresence of God. It includes such statements as:

> You hem me in—behind and before . . . .
> Where can I go from your Spirit?
> Where can I flee from your presence?
> If I go up to the heavens, you are there;
> if I make my bed in the depths, you are there.

This is supposed to be good news. Jesus later affirmed this same truth when he promised, "I am with you always." But that day this young woman transferred her feelings about her parents to her feelings about God which is, of course, entirely normal. Commenting on the Scripture, her tone was bitter: "It makes me feel watched!" Clearly she did not see God's purposes as good, and it contributed to an angry, joyless spirit.

While there is more to joy than our attitude about God, for

believers any hope of joy must involve one's perception of the heavenly Father. University professor and author Dallas Willard observes, "Our problem is not that we have not gotten what is in our head down in our heart; the problem is that we have gotten something wrong in our head and it got down in our heart" ("Spiritual Formation in Christ for the Whole Life and the Whole Person," *Vocatio*, Vol. 12, No. 2, pp. 4-7).

Getting Our Acting Together

continue to work out your salvation

Having made clear the foundation of our attitude, we must follow through with the rest of the story. To paraphrase the book of James, "Attitude without action is stillborn." Philippians 2:12-13 is not an invitation to a passive life, a cheap-grace joy. It is a call in view of the kind of God revealed in 2:5-11, to "work out" the implications of this. The transference of the character of the servant Savior of verses 5-11 makes it possible for us "to will and to act" according to God's good purpose.

Talking about obedience, Christian action and sanctification can subtly take us back to a controlling attitude. Good works can become our attempt to manipulate God, others and ourselves into acceptance. Even where obedience is concerned, God's goodness must forever remain the prime cause, the point of origin of any Christian behavior. If it does not, joy is choked.

In *What's So Amazing About Grace*, Phillip Yancey refers to French intellectual Simone Weil who concluded that two great forces rule the universe: gravity and grace. Gravity, her thinking went, causes one body to attract other bodies so that it continually enlarges by absorbing more and more of the universe. Yancey cites Adam and Eve's desire to "be as gods" as evidence of this longing to "expand, to acquire, to swell in significance." Weil saw grace as the exception to this force in nature. Yancey writes,

The Christian life, I believe, does not primarily center on ethics or rules but rather involves a new way of seeing. I escape the force of spiritual "gravity " when I begin to see myself as a sinner who cannot please God by any method of self-improvement or self-enhancement. Only then can I turn to God for outside help—for grace—and to my amazement I learn that a holy God already loves me despite my defects. I escape the force of gravity again when I recognize my neighbors also as sinners, loved by God. A grace-full Christian is one who looks at the world through "grace-tinted lenses" (p. 272).

Grace-tinted lenses enable us properly to know and cooperate (work out our salvation) with the God who works in us to will and to act according to his good purpose. The emotional/spiritual serendipity of grace-motivated obedience is joy.

Too often the gift of salvation is understood as a kind of insurance policy—Jesus made the payment and we collect the benefits. A better analogy would be to see salvation as a rehabilitation program. Jesus gives us job security, raw materials and a great retirement program. But it goes wasted if we do not "go to work" in joyful gratitude.

*that I may boast on the day of Christ that I did not
run or labor for nothing*

Deitrich Bonhoefer blasted "cheap grace" or passive salvation in his classic book *The Cost of Discipleship*. I have been deeply challenged by his declaration, ". . . only those who obey, believe" (p. 57). It reminds me of Galatians 5:6, "The only thing that counts is faith expressing itself through love." In fact, these words from Galatians set the proper relationship of faith and works: first faith, then love/obedience. Apart from this sequence, love/obedience become another attempt to "expand" our world for our sakes. While I declare in utter sincerity that I am not worthy to clean Bonhoefer's boots, I would, in fear and trembling, paraphrase his observation to say, ". . . only those who obey with joy, believe in the Christ of the Bible." (By this I do not mean a non-stop bubble bath of joy, but that often subtle, always ready to emerge awareness of God's goodness.)

Do everything without complaining or arguing, so that you may become blameless and pure, children of God without fault in a crooked and depraved generation.

Remembering the context of these verses, we recall that Christ, when he came, emptied himself of his rights as God. His example, applied to us, is a challenge to empty ourselves of any illusions of God-like adequacy. Put in simple terms, Philippians 2 tells us that Christ, as part of the Trinity, was eternally an end in himself. At a point in our time, the second member of the Trinity voluntarily gave up that status and became the means to our salvation.

The Joy of the Lord

How was Jesus able to make himself a means? Often such a question takes us back to Hebrews 12:2 where we read that Jesus endured the cross "for the sake of the joy" that it would bring. We can lay hold of joy to serve, as Jesus did, as we grasp and are grasped by the joy that the impact of obedience to God ultimately brings. And why is that so? At the center of it all is a God who loves us so much that doing or motivating others to do what is best results in his joy.

John Wesley was known to shuffle the words of Philippians 2:12 around to read, "It is God that of his good pleasure worketh in you both to will and to do." This reconstruction reveals an amazing truth: God works in our lives for good because it gives him joy! God's activity for good does not come in response to our goodness.

It comes simply because he loves us.

I discovered the depth of this in an unexpected place. One of our children was to have a major part in a musical at her college, about 10 hours away from where we live. As so often is the case, it was in the midst of a very busy time for my wife and me. Finally I was able to clear the decks for a day to travel to see the play and a day to drive home. Our daughter was happy that I could come, always glad to see someone from home and wanting to share her joy in the theatrical presentation.

That night, as the lights went down and the music began, something stirred deeply within me. When at last our daughter came on the stage, I knew why I had come. Yes, it was in part for her, to affirm her and offer a sacrificial gift of love. But something deeper was going on in my heart. As she played her part she reminded me so of her mother 25 years earlier. I felt such thankfulness for the gifts God had given our child and for her strong appropriation of those gifts. It became clear to me why I had "sacrificially" come: It filled my heart with joy to be there!

This is the motivation for the servanthood of Jesus. As we get in touch with the kind of loving God we are serving, it can become, more and more, our motivation for obedient service. It can become, too, the wellspring of joy in our lives.

But even if I am being poured out like a drink offering
I am glad and rejoice with all of you

A relevant experience is recorded in Nehemiah 8. God's people, having returned to Jerusalem, are rebuilding the city and their faith as well. They gather to hear the law of God read aloud, having let it lapse into unfamiliarity. Hearing God's Word, their hearts are struck by its truth. The stage is set for wailing and gnashing of teeth. Nehemiah, the governor, and Ezra, the priest and scribe, and the Levites who taught the people, give this remarkable instruction, 'This day is sacred to the Lord your God. Do not mourn or weep....

Do not grieve, for the joy of the Lord is your strength" (8:9,10).

Those leaders had the spiritual sense to understand that while grief and sorrow over sin is necessary, it is not the foundation for a life of faith. Our firm foundation is God, the God and Father of our Lord Jesus Christ. This is the God of joy, the God who finds joy in serving his beloved children.

Enter His Joy with Thanksgiving

The single most important truth I have learned about the practice of daily prayer is routinely to begin with praise and thanksgiving, to begin with a God worth praising. For many years I found my prayers beginning with declarations of guilt or need—either "forgive me" or "help me." While I would not exclude those cries from the opening of a time of prayer, it gradually became clear that such a beginning was an invocation of my problems, not of the presence of God. After a few minutes of confession or petition, I had spiritually screwed myself into the ground. Prayer died.

Opening prayer with praise helps plug us into the God whose joy is our strength. From that relationship, confession and petition naturally flow. They take their rightful place in the foundation of God's character.

A friend recently told me what she had concluded were two of the most important words in the Bible, "but God." As Stephen began his speech in Acts 7, he speaks of Abraham who had no inheritance of property, "but God promised him . . . ." (vs.5). In Acts 13 the apostle Paul is outlining the story of salvation. Having spoken of the cross and the burial of Jesus, he then adds, "But God raised him from the dead . . . ." (vs. 30). In Ephesians 2, Paul writes of the plight of the human race, being "dead in your transgressions and sins." Then in verse four he declares, "But (because of his great love for us), God, who is rich in mercy, made us alive with Christ . . . ."

Joy, as the Bible and the experience of believers affirms, can be found in this world because of the "but God" declarations of

Scripture that grow from what he has revealed about himself to us. As we read of the first generation of Christians, it seems that they were given that name because they were "Christ-is-here" persons. And since that was so, joy naturally followed.

For a number of years the chaplain at Dachau concentration camp, near Munich, was a man named Christian Reger. Reger himself had been a prisoner at Dachau. After a month of living in barracks built for 200 but crammed with 1,600, he found himself a hopeless man. He concluded there could be no loving God.

In July of 1941 a simple thing happened that changed his mind. His one letter for the month arrived from home. It had been snipped by the censors, but at the bottom his wife has printed the New Testament notation, Acts 4:26-29. He was able to locate a New Testament and looked up that reference. As it turned out, it was part of a speech by Peter and John after being released from prison:

> The kings of the earth take their stand, and the rulers gather together against the Lord and his anointed One. Indeed Herod and Pontius Pilate met together with the Gentiles and the people of Israel in this city to conspire against your holy servant Jesus, whom you anointed. They did what your power and will had decided beforehand should happen. Now, Lord, consider their threats and enable your servants to speak your word with great boldness.

That afternoon Reger was to be interrogated, an event greatly feared by the prisoners. As he entered the interrogation room, the man who was leaving, a fellow minister, slipped something into Reger's pocket. Nothing was said.

The interrogation was not violent, and was easier than he had feared. Returning to his bunk, nervous and sweaty with tension, he remembered the incident with the minister. Reaching in his coat pocket he found what had been placed there—a matchbox. His first thought was that it was simply a kind gesture, as matches were a priceless commodity in the barracks. Inside, however, he found no matches, only a slip of paper on which was the Bible reference, Acts 4: 26-29 (Philip Yancey, *Where Is God When It Hurts?* p. 94ff.).

Suddenly he could say, "I was in despair, but God . . . ." Christianity became Christ-is-here-ity. Joy, not giddy joy, but ocean-depth joy returned to an empty soul.

So you too should be glad and rejoice with me

Pastor Steve Sjogren tells the following true story.

On a hot, humid summer day in Cincinnati a man named Joe Delaney was playing catch with his son, Jared. Jared asked, "Dad, is there a God?" Joe replied, "I don't know." Jared continued, "Dad, if there is a God how would you know Him?" His Dad answered, "I've been to church only a time or two; I don't know about such things . . . ."

Jared continued deep in thought. Finally, he ran into the house and came back with a large helium-filled balloon he had acquired at the circus, along with some tape, a pen, and a note card. On the card he wrote these words: Dear God, if you are there and if you are real, send people who know you to Dad and me.

He taped the card to the balloon and let it go.

Two days later Joe and his son pulled into a carwash that Steve Sjogren and his congregation were staging. It was a free car wash.

When Joe asked how much it was he was told, "We do this to show the love of God in a practical way."

Joe was stunned. Then he brightened up and asked, "Wait a minute. Are you guys Christians?"

Steve replied, "Yes, we're Christians."

"The kind of Christians who believe in God?" Joe asked.

"Yes," Steve answered, "we're that kind of Christians" (*Conspiracy of Kindness*, pp. 15-17).

Do you suppose there was any joy in that exchange? Obviously. Joe and Jared and Steve had to be filled with joy. And, yes, God was probably overflowing. But, then, that's the kind of God Steve and his people believe in. And that is the kind we all can believe in, the God of joy.

French poet, novelist and playwright, Victor Hugo, wrote,

> Be like the bird that, pausing in her flight
> awhile on boughs too light
> feels them give away beneath her, and
> yet sings, knowing she has wings.

Joy

With the wings of faith outstretched, the wind of God's joy lifts our hearts. Every current eventually takes us back to Him, back to joy.

Questions for Discussion

1. What is joy?
   When you think of the church, do you think of joy? Why? Why not?

2. John Wesley said that people are not happy because they are not holy. Why would he come to that conclusion?

3. At the heart of temptation is the suggestion that we know better than God what is good for us. How does our view of God factor into this process?

4. How does the "shield" of faith protect our joy?

5. What untruths have you held about God that Jesus has corrected?

6. What is the difference between seeing salvation as insurance and seeing salvation as rehabilitation?

7. How does 1 Corinthians 13:1-3 help define the deeper nature of the mind of Christ?

8. Have there been any "but God" experiences in your life? Explain.

CHAPTER NINE

Going off the Shallow End

Philippians 3:1-9

Finally, my brothers, rejoice in the Lord! It is no trouble for me to write the same things to you again, and it is a safeguard for you. Watch out for those dogs, those men who do evil, those mutilators of the flesh. For it is we who are the circumcision, we who worship by the Spirit of God, who glory in Christ Jesus, and who put no confidence in the flesh—though I myself have reasons for such confidence. If anyone else thinks he has reasons to put confidence in the flesh, I have more: circumcised on the eighth day, of the people of Israel, of the tribe of Benjamin, a Hebrew of Hebrews; in regard to the law, a Pharisee; as for zeal, persecuting the church; as for legalistic righteousness, faultless. But whatever was to my profit I now consider loss for the sake of Christ. What is more, I consider everything a loss compared to the surpassing greatness of knowing Christ Jesus my Lord, for whose sake I have lost all things. I consider them rubbish, that I may gain Christ and be found in him, not having a righteousness of my own that comes from the law, but that which is through faith in Christ—the righteousness that comes from God and is by faith.

Have you ever "childproofed" a house? There are a couple of reasons to take such measures. One motive is to protect the home of its breakable items. Most parents know the tension of visiting someone's home who owns fragile figurines. I have a chilling memory of one of our children, as we visited with friends, sailing a china butterfly across the room. We learned to go ahead and ask hosts to put fragile things out of reach.

The other side of the childproofing coin is a concern for the welfare of the child. What parent doesn't know the anxiety of asking a small child how many pills he or she has swallowed, or trying to remember how much cough syrup was in the now empty bottle the last time it was used. It is logical that another term for one who takes responsibility for children is *guardian*.

Moving on through the letter to the Philippians, we find Paul acting as a guardian to this young church, tending to matters of community, encouraging the fellowship to receive gladly Timothy and Epaphroditus. In the midst of weighty cosmic matters, Paul genuinely cares about individuals and practical pastoral relationships.

Having done a little fence-mending, he returns to serious theological issues, focusing on a kind of spiritual childproofing of the household of faith. But it is not as simple as hiding the heirlooms or locking up the medicines. His burden is to remove spiritually toxic attitudes, which if ingested in a young Christian's life, could prove fatal.

With the intensity of a parent ripping the rat poison from his/her child's hand, the great apostle wastes no time in banishing the threat to his spiritual children. Up to this point, the tone of the letter has been gentle, but now a state of war is declared.

> *Watch out for those dogs, those men who do evil,*
> *those mutilators of the flesh*

Learning Christian Math

What is this great threat? I wish I could tell you something you had never heard, something new and intriguing. But it is not new. The grave danger they faced was this—wanting to add something to the cross of Jesus Christ as necessary to salvation.

As old hat as this may sound, had they done it, you would not be reading these words today. The Christian movement would have blended into the Jewish faith and/or simply disappeared. So for the sake of the household of faith, Paul leaps to a defensive position. It was not a fragile decoration that was in danger. It was the essence of the gospel. With concern for the heart of the faith, he simultaneously seeks to protect the "children" of the household of faith.

We might imagine him, were he present in our time, asking these kinds of questions:

- Are you attempting to add to the saving work of Jesus Christ?
- Do you find yourself trying to hedge your bets with certain works, rituals?
- What is your primary motive as a Christian—fear or gratitude?

Wherever Paul went he declared what had been so clearly affirmed to the Ephesian church: "We are saved by grace, through faith, and this is not from yourselves, it is a gift of God, not by works, so that no one can boast" (2:8-9). It was and is a message that human pride finds disagreeable.

A painfully simple issue precipitated the words of Philippians 3—the desire of some former Jews to include circumcision as an essential component of the new covenant. This seems to us like much ado about nothing. The fact that it seems so inconsequential confirms the truth of the observation: if you are suffering, it is so someone else will not have to; if you are not suffering, it is because someone else has.

Since the apostle Paul suffered the persecution of legalistic believers, the message of salvation by grace through faith was passed on to succeeding generations. Out of his struggle we received the clear teaching of the New Testament that we are saved by *Christ plus nothing*.

A woman was arguing with her pastor about this business of faith and works.

"I think that getting to heaven is like rowing a boat. One oar is faith and the other is works. If you use both, you get there."

The pastor replied, "There is only one thing wrong with your illustration. *Nobody is going to heaven in a row boat*" (W. Wiersbey, *Be Joyful*, p. 94).

Hear the questions again: Are you are trying to add anything to the efficacy of the work of Christ? Do you think you need another oar to put into the water to make it to the other shore?

Paul was hounded by a Jewish group known as Judaizers. These religious people were so angry at the teaching of salvation by grace through faith that 40 of them took a vow not to eat or drink until Paul had been killed (Acts 23). Obviously, this was not a friendly disagreement. Paul was willing to risk his life to preserve this faith. He minces no words, calling these Judaizers dogs, mutilators of the flesh. The church is warned to avoid them like the plague. Supplementing the gift of grace was clearly understood by Paul as the beginning of a slippery slope back into the old covenant.

Charles Wesley, whose hymns impart a message of salvation by grace through faith, had not always understood what Paul fought here to protect. In late February of 1738, on the doorstep of the as-yet-unimagined Wesleyan revival, Charles had a conversation that exposed his inner wrestlings with grace. He had been bedridden with pleurisy and was occasionally visited by an earnest young Moravian Christian named Peter Bohler. That day as their conversation turned to spiritual things, Bohler asked Charles to explain what reasons he had for hoping to be saved. He answered, "Because I have used my best endeavors to serve God." Peter Bohler said nothing in response, but shook his head in obvious disappointment. After his visitor left, Charles recorded the exchange in his Journal, adding these words, "I thought him very uncharitable, saying in my heart, 'What, are not my endeavors a sufficient ground of hope? Would he rob me of my endeavors? I have nothing else to trust to'" (*The Message of the Wesleys*, Philip Watson, p. 1).

Some of Paul's opponents might well have said of him, "Would he rob us of our heritage reflected in circumcision? We have nothing else to trust." This was not an unreasonable position to take before the events of Holy Week. Now, there was something else, Someone else to trust in. That Someone had radically altered the spiritual landscape by his obedient life and death. The Father substantiated that by raising him from the dead, a singular attestation to the singular significance of Jesus. Paul had ridden on the rocket of grace and was not about to go back to peddling the stationary bike of good works and ritualistic practices. It was a paradigm shift that many others would need to make in the centuries to follow.

Isn't That Enough?

*If anyone else thinks he has reasons to put
confidence in the flesh, I have more*

Sam Shoemaker, one of the leading lights of Alcoholics Anonymous and the Faith at Work movement, went to Princeton, planning to become an Episcopal priest. An opportunity came up to go to China with a YMCA missions group. While in that far-away land he began to feel a spiritual lack, becoming aware in a new way of his own deep-seated selfishness. Wrestling with his calling at a deeper level than before, he found himself saying to God, "I am going into the ministry—isn't that enough?" (*I Stand by the Door*, p. 25)

Sound familiar? I'm:

teaching Sunday school…
singing in the choir
tithing
putting up with _____
not _____
You fill in the blank _____

Isn't that enough?
How does this compute with Christ plus nothing?
"Isn't that enough?" sounds like the poster slogan for the "righteousness through the law" approach to salvation. The weakness is obvious: the answer is always, "No." Perhaps this is why Woody Allen spoke of Judaism as "guilt with holidays."
In this section of Philippians (3:1-9) Paul reels off his pedigree,

and it is impressive. Seminary professor and author Fred Craddock was right on the money when he said of Paul, ". . . he could preach the Judaizers' sermon better than they" (*Interpretation—Philippians*, p. 57). Two statements grabbed my attention in Paul's simultaneous self-affirmation and categorical rejection of human abilities to satisfy God's holiness:

> (3:6b) "...as for legalistic righteousness, faultless."
> (3:9) "...not having a righteousness of my own that comes from the law, but that which is through faith in Christ. . . . ."

What is obvious here is that Paul's understanding of righteousness was transformed by Jesus Christ. There is clearly a kind of righteousness, the limits to which Paul now understood, that springs from an equation involving God's law and obedience to it. While most of us cannot claim, as did Paul, that we are faultless in this category, there are a few Olympian souls who maintain amazingly moral lives. Sir Lancelot is initially presented as this sort of saint in the musical *Camelot*, singing with gusto, "I'm blessed with an iron will. Had I been made the partner of Eve, we'd be in Eden still!" *Camelot* ends as a story about humankind's fatal flaw, and Lancelot is right in the middle of the mess.

No, It's Not Enough

Paul, however, seems to have truly been an iron-willed individual, which is what so perfectly qualified him to understand and expose the shortcomings of such righteousness. He could freely declare its limits with no appearance of doing so as the rationalization of an immoral life.

He stands in the same old covenant line as the rich young man (Mark 10) who said of "the commandments," ". . . all these I have kept since I was a boy." We also see in Paul a similar spirit as the elder brother of the prodigal son. The elder one was a righteous man, but it did not seem to unite him to his father. And that is the point. That is why a higher form of righteousness, of obedience, is needed, a righteousness based on holy love, ". . . that which is through faith in Christ—the righteousness that comes from God and is by faith" (3: 9b).

not having a righteousness of my own that comes from the law,
but that which is through faith in Christ

I am not a Christian from the Calvinist tradition. (I know there are many varieties of understanding within that tradition.) Like John Wesley, however, I am but a "hair's breadth" from it. I do believe in predestination. Jesus was predestined to be the Savior. By grace through faith I am able to participate in his election as the Chosen One. In himself he became the new Israel, the priest linking God and humankind. Now "in Christ" I share in his righteousness.

Where I, and I believe Wesley as well, generally line up with Calvin is in his understanding that we are lost as a race apart from God's gracious initiative. That includes every human being who ever has lived or will live. Sixteenth-century Englishman John Bradford was apparently the source of the well-known expression, "There but for the grace of God go I." He spoke it as prisoners were led off for execution. A strict Calvinist would interpret this to mean that Bradford understood God's sovereign, arbitrary choice to save him as the reason for his law-abiding life. Wesley would say that *every* person is given the choice to receive or reject grace by which to make subsequent choices of obedience. He did not so much believe in free will as in free grace, which creates the possibility of moral choice in human experience.

Wesley believed that if the exercising of human will was taken out of the salvation equation, the eventual result was moral passivity, which he saw all around him. That power of choice, however, is not intended to be seen as a reason for human pride. Wesley, too, would clearly affirm, "There but for the grace of God giving me the possibility of saying "Yes" to God, go I."

This is a mystery, to be sure.

There is scripture that supports almost any stripe on this continuum. My contention in walking through this theological minefield is simple: Calvinist or Wesleyan/Arminian teaching alike, both ultimately place their trust in God's grace, not human merit. At least that is what our doctrine says.

> *I consider them rubbish . . . not having*
> *a righteousness that comes from the law*

The question is, what about everyday life? Don't we still reveal our inner mixture of grace and pride as we look down on other people?

the out of wedlock mother,
the welfare cheat,
dishonest politicians,
conservatives/liberals/moderates/progressives,
the poor/the rich,
the homely/the beautiful,
televangelists/criminals.

Don't we actually think, "There but for the grace of God, *and the fact that I am a better person than he*, go I."

This is why there is so little joy in many Christians. We know we aren't perfect, but we refuse to hit bottom, where we would find the real meaning of grace and the freedom and blessing it brings. My brothers, rejoice in the Lord! It is no trouble to me to write the same things to you again, and it is a safeguard for you.

Amazing Grace

Read, with a little running commentary added in, Ephesians 2:1, 3b-4,

"As for you, you were dead in your transgressions and sins.... [How dead is dead? Can you be a little dead or mostly dead, but not quite all dead?] Like the rest, we were by nature objects of wrath [but some deserve it a lot more than we do]. But because of his great love for us [and the fact that we are nice people?], God, who is rich in mercy, made us alive with Christ even when we were dead in transgressions [Dead? Didn't we help a little? No, so I am going to say it again]—it is by grace you have been saved."

If Jesus were to take over at this point I strongly suspect that he would back away from the theological talk of this chapter and use a story to illustrate how this all fits together. One of the best examples I have read was shared by M. Craig Barnes, former pastor of National Presbyterian Church in Washington.

When Barnes was a child, his father, a pastor, brought home a 12-year-old boy named Roger. Roger's parents had both died from drug overdoses. No one else seemed willing to help Roger, so the Barnes family took him in. Roger became a "joint heir" in the family and lived with them until he grew up and joined the Army.

While this was a great boon for Roger, it also meant a lot of new effort in his life. Moving from a home overseen by heroin addicts to a committed Christian family led to continuous culture shock. Roger, accustomed to screaming and fighting, had to learn new ways of relating to the family. Constantly stoned parents left Roger driven by fear, wondering about his next meal. In his new home many lessons were to be learned about sharing, good manners and chores.

Barnes asks, "Was any of Roger's hard work to change behavior necessary in order to be part of the family?" The answer was "no." The grace with which Craig's parents had adopted Roger began on day one. But change was still necessary. And that change was fostered in an unchanging atmosphere of love.

We are all like Roger when we enter God's family through his adoptive grace. The changes at which we must work (repentance) are not undertaken to assure our status as God's children, but because we are God's children. "That's not how you act in this family." How often does the Holy Spirit send that message to us? Very often. In the Father's un-earnable and freely given love we can find the power to change.

Roger, like my brother, was killed in Vietnam. In his new Christian home, he had seen modeled that greater love that lays down its life for a friend. Commenting on his parents' loving, daily efforts to re-form Roger's wounded life, Barnes writes, "Through it all, they were teaching him how to live out his identity as a cherished son" (*Sacred Thirst*, pp. 91-92). This is the story of a life saved by grace.

And Again I Say, Rejoice!

It is illuminating, having slogged through this theological marsh, to return to the benign sounding words of the beginning of chapter three: "Finally, my brothers, rejoice in the Lord. It is no trouble for me to write the same things to you again, and it is a safeguard for you." In childproofing the household of faith, Paul begins with the spirit of worship. The spirit of worship is a way of seeing, looking at life with the eyes of the heart. While I cannot recall who said it, I have never forgotten these haunting words, "I looked into the heart of a saint. I never want to look into the heart of a sinner." Whoever it was must have looked with the eyes of his own heart.

It is natural for our pride to go off the shallow end and then wonder why our worship, our joy, our wonder, seem so limited. The shallow end is the place where we still live with the illusion that we are saved by anything other than the pure gift of God's mercy. We never experience the depths of joy, of worship, until we face the depths of our need. It is likely, too, that our service and our love, will be shallow so long as we remain in the shallows of self-knowledge.

*I consider everything a loss compared to the surpassing
greatness of knowing Jesus Christ my Lord*

In the seventh chapter of Luke is a story of Jesus being anointed by a "sinful" woman in the home of a Pharisee. (This appears to be a different incident from the anointing recorded in the other three gospels near the time of Jesus' death.) It is loaded with theological implications, some subtle, some akin to a sledgehammer.

One of the latter possibilities is the action of Jesus in pronouncing pardon upon this woman, thus directly claiming a divine prerogative. That was a bold, daring thing for Jesus to do, especially in the home of a Pharisee. It is one of those behaviors on Jesus' part that appears to affirm his self-understanding as being more than only a human prophet.

Another brief but blazing theological moment occurs at the end of the story when Jesus says, "Your faith has saved you; go in peace." Jesus clearly implies that it was not the woman's deed that brought her pardon. It was the faith that motivated the deed. Faith has always had the power to arrest the attention of God, however it manifests itself. The woman's action did not suddenly make her meritorious in the Lord's eyes. Her faith gave him the freedom to extend forgiveness and peace, which has its source in him.

With regard to our concern in this portion of Philippians, Jesus' most important words come in the form of an elementary equation—the extent of forgiveness equals the depth of developing love in the heart of the forgiven. The greater one's understanding of the need for grace, the greater one's potential for grateful love.

We should probably cut Simon, the Pharisee in whose house this took place, some slack for even allowing this woman in the door. But his grace seems to end there. She is publicly categorized, as would have been common at the time, as "a sinner" (7:39). This prompts Jesus to get out a velvet-covered brick and throw it at his host. He does so through a simple story about two men in debt to the same moneylender. One owes considerably more than the other. Both are forgiven their debts. Jesus concludes with the simple question: "Now which of them will love him more?"

Simon, cautiously, offers the obvious answer, "I suppose the one who had the bigger debt canceled." Jesus then proceeds to point out that upon his entering Simon's house, not even the customary water for washing dusty feet was offered, but this woman has done the job with her tears and hair, providing sweet-smelling perfume to enhance the cleansing process. Jesus interpreted her action, not as manipulation to win his approval, but as gratitude for his gracious spirit. He then concludes, "But he who has been forgiven little loves little." It is uncertain whether or not Simon was aware of the large bulls'-eye that Jesus saw on Simon when he said those words.

Simon loved little.

Was it because he was in less need of grace as this woman? Be careful as you answer that question. Your answer may determine the freedom and joy in your life. Your answer may have a direct impact on the place of self-righteousness in your life.

Simon loved little because his understanding of his own need for grace was so feeble. Jesus was already working on childproofing the household of faith from the toxins brought on by blind self-righteousness and shallow righteousness.

> *not having a righteousness of my own that comes from the law,*
> *but that which is through faith in Christ—*
> *the righteousness that comes from God and is by faith.*

That Saved A Wretch Like Me

God is using a powerful voice to the same end these days with the ministry of Episcopal preacher, Fleming Rutledge. Her messages "do not suffer spiritual fools like Simon." She shares out of the experience of recognizing her own profound need for grace in the everyday affairs of life. One example concerns a day on which she was driving toward a certain destination and made several wrong turns. This resulted in her getting so far off course that it took half an hour to get right again. Then she made another mistake trying to get on an interstate highway. Suddenly, as it usually happens while driving at highway speed, she saw an opportunity to set things right. The only problem was that in order to do so she would need to make an illegal turn, a turn clearly prohibited by a plainly visible road sign. What did she do? She did what most of us would do. She looked to see if there were any police in sight, quickly surveyed the scene, sped up and started to change lanes to make the forbidden turn. What was the result? By her estimation, having failed to see an on-coming car in the other lane, she missed a broadside collision by a fraction of an inch, swerving at the last second. Needless to say the driver of the other car revealed his need for grace in his expressions of "dismay" to her.

In hearing her repeat this story, people usually say to her, "That's not sin!" They make excuses for her: fatigue, just a mistake, momentary stupidity, but not *sin*.

Listen to her telling response to such attempts to rescue her.

> In this episode on the highway, we see how deeply ingrained certain attitudes are within the human being. In making the forbidden left turn, I had acted upon the assumption that the rules did not apply to me. I did not take the proper precautions. I put other lives in danger. I did not think of what it might mean to my family if I were killed. I put my own wishes ahead of the common good. Perhaps worst of all I presumed upon God's mercy. These traits are so deeply imbedded in human personality that we scarcely think about them (*Help My Unbelief*, pp. 130-31).

"We scarcely think about them." We Christians who enjoy prosperity can spend hundreds of dollars on clothes, thousands of dollars on vacations, tens of thousands of dollars on vehicles, many tens of thousands on our children's education and hundreds of thousands on houses, and scarcely think about the millions who live on less than hundreds per year. Is this *sin*?

I know. We can rationalize all of it. The rationalization is part of the sin. Yes, no one wants to hear this. But the amazing and absolutely required grace of God loses its glory unless we see the depth of our need. When we finally begin to see it, we realize what English Christian apologist Os Guinness meant when he said that disciples are not people who follow Jesus. They are people who *must* follow Jesus. Otherwise, we are without hope.

The great Bible expositor Alexander Maclaren said, "The Bible can venture to give full weight to the gravity of sickness because it knows the remedy" (quoted in Rutledge, p. 178).

Paul returns to that remedy before the conclusion of Philippians with some of Scripture's most beautiful and hopeful words. In chapter three we observe Paul's self-evaluation which is also apparent in Acts 20: 27, ". . . I have not hesitated to proclaim to you the whole will of God." His concern is the same as that expressed in 2 Corinthians 6:1, "As God's fellow workers, we urge you not to receive God's grace in vain."

In the second chapter of Galatians Paul uses this same expression in reference to a visit to church leaders in Jerusalem, where the gospel message was the topic of discussion. There the word of salvation by grace through faith was confirmed. In fact the very issue of circumcision was addressed. The outcome? "This matter arose, because some false brothers had infiltrated our ranks to spy on the freedom we have in Christ Jesus and to make us slaves. We did not give in to them for a moment, so that the truth of the gospel might remain with you" (2:4-5).

For it is we who are the circumcision,
we who worship by the Spirit of God, who glory in Christ Jesus,
and who put no confidence in the flesh

Christians everywhere should be grateful that Paul did not give in for a moment. As a result the truth of the gospel remains with us to this day.

Questions for Discussion

1. Define and/or describe Christian faith.

2. What is the relationship in a Christian believer's life between fear of God and gratitude to God?

3. In what are you trusting for salvation? Why?

4. Why did the righteousness of the prodigal son's elder brother not connect him to his father's heart?

5. What does it mean to say that free will is founded on free grace?

6. What does the story about Roger tell us about the relationship of grace and works?

7. How are healthy self-love and forgiveness related? Does this have any bearing on why self-righteous people tend to "love little"?

8. If the shallow end of faith is driven by works, what would be the driving force in the deep end? What joy is found in the deep end that would not be found in the shallow end?

CHAPTER TEN

Know, Know, Know-Reaching out to Know Jesus Christ

Philippians 3:10-16

I want to know Christ and the power of his resurrection and the fellowship of his sufferings, becoming like him in his death, and so, somehow, to attain to the resurrection from the dead.

Not that I have already obtained all this, or have already been made perfect, but I press on to take hold of that for which Christ Jesus took hold of me.

Brothers, I do not consider myself yet to have taken hold of it. But one thing I do: Forgetting what is behind and straining toward what is ahead,

I press on toward the goal to win the prize for which God has called me heavenward in Christ Jesus.

All of us who are mature should take such a view of things.

And if on some point you think differently, that too God will make clear to you.

Only let us live up to what we have already attained.

Remember the old joke about the mountain man who enrolled his teenage son in school? When he was told that one of the subjects was trigonometry, he said, "Good, give him plenty of that trigger-nometry. He's a lousy shot!"

These verses in chapter three bring us to a similar-sounding subject known in philosophy as epistemology (you know—e-pistol-mology). Epistemology is the subject of "knowing." How do we know anything? Is life an illusion, fabricated in our gray matter? Are *we* real? How do we know?

This sort of abstract thinking is a sign that we are "fearfully and wonderfully made" (Psalm 139:14). Our amazing minds are capable of flirting with the infinite. Confronting mind-bending philosophical questions can be a rigorous adventure that fearfully and wonderfully explores the limits of our mental and spiritual capacities. It can also become an intellectual gerbil wheel, vigorous in its motions but immobile in its progress. Perhaps you recall a typical question from Philosophy 101: "If people believe life is all in their heads, why don't they meditate while sitting on railroad tracks?" In spite of the ability of the mind to "write checks that reality can't sign," we still have a hunger to *know that what we know* is real.

English lay theologian G. K. Chesterton observed that the purpose of opening the mind is akin to opening the mouth to eat—the whole point is eventually to close it on something *solid*.

Garbage Out—Jesus In

The apostle Paul,
a world-class thinker in any generation,
with all the benefits of rabbinical education,
travel, and profound spiritual experience,
had been confronted by something,
Someone, he considered to be incomparably *solid*,
Someone he wanted to know thoroughly.

Paul had already described his former ways of knowing God as garbage, or *having lost its value* in comparison. That is extreme language. This is extremely important to Paul. In Philippians 3:12 and following, confessing both his failure and his faith, he reaffirms that what is behind him, his former way of relating to God, is as good as forgotten. What remains is a life with hands outstretched, straining toward what is ahead. He is not straining to achieve but straining to believe. There is no bragging of his victories, only of the One on Whom he is focused.

The *New Revised Standard Version* renders 3:12 "Not that I have already obtained this [knowing Christ, knowing the power of Christ's resurrection and the fellowship of His suffering] or have already reached the goal; but I press on to make it my own, *because Christ Jesus has made me his own*" (italics mine). This pressing on is not the same as earlier efforts at faithfulness. The knowledge that Paul seeks will not yield itself to him because of his righteous behavior. His former compulsion that drove him like a member of a Jewish gestapo to track down Christians—such works righteousness—is now *useless*. This new pursuit grows out of the grace inherent in the Savior and Lord who has taken the initiative to make us his own. By faith Paul is working out what it means to keep our spiritual hands empty, our pride under our heel like a threatening serpent, to receive what God freely gives. The prize toward which he reaches is the utterly unique and categorically unparalleled "heavenly call" God has issued through his Son.

I press on to take hold of that for which Christ Jesus took hold of me

With transparent passion, Paul announces his new life goal, the pursuit of which is possible because of Christ Jesus Who in dynamic grace has taken hold of him—to know Christ, the power of his resurrection, and the fellowship of His suffering.

Early in this letter we have a foreshadowing of this longing when he affirms, "For me to live is Christ" (1:21). In chapter two, Paul fleshes this out as the words of verses 6-11 witness to the humble, human particularity of Christ Jesus. In other words, "for me to live is to walk by faith in Christ Jesus who relinquished his rights as God, obediently suffered to the point of death, was exalted by God, and now is Lord, revealing God's glory [paraphrase mine]." What a contrast of soul to the Saul of Acts 9:1, "still breathing out murderous threats." No wonder he saw his former disposition as garbage.

Here in chapter three Paul moves beyond speaking of Jesus Christ as a noble standard by which to live or a dramatic example to follow or even a Lord before whom he would bow. This Christ Jesus is One with whom we may share the kind of yoked relationship experienced by close acquaintances. The "mind of Christ" we are told in chapter two to have among us is not only a way of thinking, but it also is a predisposition toward God the Father—a relationship of trusting obedience—which enables the Father to bless a life as the Christ hymn of 2:6-11 declares.

Can we really know God? Jesus, who shared our humanity, obviously did. Could it be that his "mind" in us, in the mystery of grace, can facilitate some degree of this knowledge?

Theologian J. I. Packer wrote a widely-read book on the topic of knowing God. In an early chapter he relates a comment made by a scholar whose views on justification by faith had set up a clash among church leaders. This scholar came to understand that his thinking on the subject had effectively ended his prospects of academic advancement. At length he said, "But it doesn't matter, for I've known God and they haven't" (*Knowing God*, p. 20). That comment broke ground for a fertile period of reflection and study in Dr. Packer's life.

Some of that thought process took him to this section of Philippians. There he was struck with the unbridled force of Paul's witness. What more extreme value could Paul place on this matter of knowing Jesus Christ than to say, "I consider *everything* a loss compared to the surpassing greatness of knowing Christ Jesus my Lord, for whose sake I have lost all things" (3: 8). Without reservation Paul unhesitatingly declares that nothing in this world compares to knowing Jesus Christ. *Nothing.* Knowing Christ Jesus is *unsurpassed*, in a category, a universe, all by itself.

Not Just Theological Correctness

Dr. Packer takes pains to clarify that this knowledge of the Savior and Lord of all should not be confused with knowledge about him or knowledge about godliness.

Having studied at seminaries on both sides of the center of the theological continuum, I can attest that knowledge about religious ideas, which "puffs up" (I Corinthians 8:1), is a danger to Christians at more than one point on the theological spectrum.

From the perspective of theological education to the right of center, where "talking the talk" can easily be mistaken for spiritual maturity, Dr. Packer affirms, "A little knowledge of God is worth more than a great deal of knowledge about Him" (p. 21). The Pharisees, the conservatives of their day, had plenty of knowledge about God.

In one seminary I attended, whose direction from center can be identified in their references to the magazine *Christianity Today* as *Christianity Yesterday*, I took a philosophy class that met for three hours one night each week of the semester. There was a break in the middle of the three-hour period. One evening, sitting in my seat during the break, I overheard two other students discussing their future. One was saying that he thought he would go on to further schooling and possibly teach on the college level. The other student asked this young divine, as seminary students were once called, if he had considered the pastoral ministry (these were Master of Divinity students). He replied, "What, and give up my Sundays?"

Theological thinking of any stripe can and usually does create a subculture. That mini-world easily becomes the bushel of which Jesus spoke that hides the light of "knowing Christ, the power of his resurrection and the fellowship of his sufferings." 1 Corinthians 13, the so-called love chapter, is a warning against such baskets that pass for Christ-knowledge, but fail the test of "re-presenting" Christ. Paul was an authority on the knowledge that puffs up. He had clearly seen its hidden hypocrisy, it counterfeit righteousness. Now he wanted to boast only of the things that showed his utter reliance on Christ (2 Corinthians 11 & 12). This is not the sort of knowledge that we "have"; it is the kind of knowledge that "has us." Hence Paul's expression, "I press on to take hold of that for which Christ Jesus took hold of me" (3:12b).

I want to know Christ

In my spiritual tradition it is said that Christian knowledge comes from four sources: scripture, tradition, reason and experience. This is referred to as "the quadrilateral." While it appears to be a comprehensive assortment of possible sources, it raises a mountain of epistemological questions. Dr. William Abraham of the Perkins School of Theology has observed two important difficulties.

The first problem the quadrilateral raises is the breadth of knowledge needed to fulfill its promise. Recently while driving on a long trip I heard a radio preacher use an old idea to refute those who claim there is no God. "Draw a circle to create a pie chart," he said. "Then, assuming this circle represents all the knowledge in the world, create a slice of the pie that represents all that you know of all the world's knowledge." He went on to say that most people, in his experience with this picture, just put a small dot somewhere in the circle, depicting the dramatic limits of their knowledge. When the unbeliever has admitted his limitations, one asks the question, "Do you suppose it is possible that God exists in that portion of knowledge you do not possess?" The most this illustration would likely do to a true unbeliever is move him from atheist to agnostic. But it points to the problem with the scope of the quadrilateral. As Dr. Abraham notes, in reality only God could meaningfully use it, as only God knows all the possibilities of the four components.

The second problem arises in the practical arena of using the elements of the quadrilateral to make decisions. Dr. Abraham writes,

> The quadrilateral, even in its most carefully stated form, does not show us how we are to resolve potential conflicts between the various sources. It is naive to think that, in a conflict between, say, scripture and reason, scripture will be allowed to carry the day. Equally, in a conflict between, say, tradition and experience, it is difficult to see how tradition will survive if it is seen in conflict with experience. The

history of modern theology shows all too clearly that reason
and experience win every time over against scripture and
tradition" (*Waking from Doctrinal Amnesia*, p. 63).

I recall hearing Dr. Abraham say that the tendency is to make a
"lateral pass" in theological decision making. If scripture did not
say what is desired, make a lateral to tradition. If tradition did
not affirm what is wanted, make a lateral to reason. If reason does
not satisfy, then you can always find experience to support your
beliefs. This approach has worked well on issues from slavery to
homosexuality.

It might justifiably be argued that this trick was learned from
scripture interpretation, moving from one passage to the next until
one's opinion is supported. Indeed, holding to the primacy of
scripture does not resolve all the possible abuses.

A second concern, which this portion of Philippians magnificently
undermines, is the possibility of seeing "knowledge" of Jesus as a
mark of superiority over others rather than the way of the cross.
Ever mindful of our flesh, we must recognize this as yet another
opportunity for pride to substitute all manner of deeds and spiritual
gifts and head-knowledge for the reality of humbly walking by faith
in the love of God (1 Corinthians 13). One of the major battles
the church faced early on was the problem of those who claimed
a superior "knowledge" or *gnosis* of Christ. This created a class of
super-spiritual folks who have been represented in some form or
fashion in the church ever since.

Such spiritual hubris calls to mind Matthew 20: 20-28 where the
mother of Zebedee's boys asked Jesus if her sons could sit on his
right and left when he came into his kingdom. Jesus asked, "Can
you drink the cup I am going to drink," or "do you understand the
nature of the glory associated with knowing Me?" When the rest
of the disciples heard about this request, they were indignant. Jesus
took it as an opportunity to say, ". . . whoever wants to become
great among you must be your servant." This takes us back to

Philippians 2, the mind of Christ, as the humble attitude of the heart in knowing Jesus.

> *and the power of his resurrection and the fellowship of his sufferings,*
> *becoming like him in his death, and so, somehow,*
> *to attain the resurrection of the dead*

Jesus—a Presence Beyond Our Knowledge

When we consider what it means to "know Christ," there is a modern biography that gracefully addresses both the possibility of meeting Jesus today and the primacy of scripture in this encounter. This story can be found in the book *Journey into Light*, the theological pilgrimage of Emile Cailliet.

Emile Cailliet was a native Frenchman (later a United States citizen), a professor at Princeton and authority on Blaise Pascal. Calliet did not see a Bible until he was 23 years old. Brought up with totally naturalistic, secular presuppositions about life, his experience as a soldier in World War I led to questions such as, "Who am I?" and "*What* am I?" Recovering from a bullet wound in an American hospital, he met and married a Scotch-Irish girl who was a Christian believer. He made it clear to her that religion would be taboo in their home.

His days of intense reflection while literally under fire created in him a deep longing. He hungered to find the "book that would understand me." Knowing of no such book, keen thinker that he was, he determined to create it himself. While reading in the course of graduate studies, he made wide-ranging notes, compiling them slowly into a notebook that would speak to his condition.

Finally, it was finished. On a beautiful day he went out and sat under a tree to read through his precious anthology. As he read, a growing disappointment came over him. The realization struck him that this effort would fail "simply because it was of my own making."

At that same moment, his wife appeared at the gate of the

garden. She knew nothing of his project. As she pushed the baby stroller through the gate, she hesitatingly shared the events of her afternoon stroll. Still not knowing the town well, she had simply gone from one street to another, eventually taking refuge from the bumpy cobblestone lanes by retreating to a patch of grass beyond a small archway. The grass led her to the doorway of a long room. After entering, she saw a cross and realized she was in the office area of a church, a Huguenot (Protestant) church. Approaching an old gentleman she soon realized to be the priest, she found herself asking, "Do you have a Bible in French?" At this point in the story she became hesitant, not wanting to anger her husband, wanting him to know this had not been planned.

"A Bible, you say? Where is it? Show me. I have never seen one before!"

He "chanced" to open it to the Beatitudes. In the desert of his longing, it seemed he had found a life-giving pool from which to drink. It hit him: this was the Book that would understand him.

He writes,

> And lo and behold, as I looked through them, the One of whom they spoke, the One who spoke and acted in them, became alive to me. . . . A decisive insight flashed through my whole being the following morning as I probed the opening chapters of the gospel according to John. The very clue to the secret of human life was disclosed right there, not stated in the foreboding language of philosophy, but in the common, everyday language of human circumstances. And far from moving on their own accord, these circumstances seemed to yield themselves without striving, obedient unto One who inexorably stood out from the gospel narrative— indeed a Person of far more than human nature and stature (p. 18).

Cailliet describes his knowledge of Jesus Christ in terms

of being aware, not just of the existence of God, but of the Presence of God.

the power of his resurrection

In my own experience, this captures the essence of coming into an initial personal knowledge of Jesus Christ. New Year's Eve, following my graduation from high school, I was about to begin college, having worked in the fall to earn money for school. I attended a Watch Night service, which culminated in Holy Communion as the New Year was welcomed in. There had been no preaching, just some readings. It seemed very dry.

All of my high school years I had prayed for God's will to be done, having concluded that God must know better than I. But I was essentially ignorant of who Jesus was, astoundingly so as I look back on it. Even so, I had felt a call to the pastoral ministry and was following this call as best I knew.

As I sat there that night, waiting to go forward for the sacrament, in my mind I heard a voice speak, a strange voice, unlike a usual "thought." The voice said, "I am here and I am alive." That was it. I didn't think, "Praise the Lord! I've met Jesus! I've been born again!" Such talk was simply not a part of who I was or of my understanding. But in the days that followed an awareness dawned that has been the most crucial realization of my life. The next time I read the Gospels, when Jesus was mentioned or spoke, it was as if I were reading about someone I had met. I know of no other way to describe it.

Since that night my prayers have been like talking to an acquaintance. No, I had not looked for this, other than indirectly by seeking God's will. But having been taken hold of by Christ, it has made all the difference ever since. His prevenient contact has motivated my desire to know more through various means of grace—scripture, prayer, fellowship with other believers and obedient service. Oswald Chambers said, "My spiritual history must have as its underlying foundation a personal knowledge of Jesus Christ. To be born again means that I see Jesus" (*My Utmost for His Highest—An Updated Version in Today's Language*, August 15 entry). I simply say, "Amen." Since that night I have been on a pilgrimage to abide in Christ, know him more, and fulfill the closing words of 2 Peter, "But grow in the grace and knowledge of our Lord and Savior Jesus Christ. To him be glory both now and forever! Amen."

I think of the image of Jesus found in Revelation 3:20, "I stand at the door and knock. If anyone hears my voice and opens the door, I will come in and eat with him and he with me." These are words that describe a personal, intimate knowledge of God in Jesus Christ. In the years since that New Year's Eve, my experience agrees with Emile Cailliet's observation, "In the last analysis, we know Him for the simple reason that He makes Himself known to us, our supreme knowledge of Him being in the awareness of His Presence in the context of an authoritative Bible" (p. 89).

Regardless of our interior experiences, knowing Jesus Christ has as its foundation and compass the scripture. As you read Paul's letters, you realize that the Hebrew scriptures had already assumed such a place of revelation for the first followers of the Way. In my devotions I have lately been using *Christ in the Psalms* by Patrick Reardon. It has been surprising to see how reading the Psalms as if they were from the lips of Jesus opens entirely new relevancies in otherwise familiar words.

The "front door" into knowledge of Jesus Christ is the Bible. To hide these words in our hearts is to know more and more fully the living Word whom it uniquely reveals. From within that door Jesus knocks, bidding us come in to know him better. I know as I write these words that, like the blind men and the elephant, knowing Jesus is vast in its potential.

Not that I have already obtained all this,
or have already been made perfect, but I press on

Journalist and commentator Bill Moyers speaking on the theme, "Let's Get Jesus Back," at Riverside Church in New York City railed against the "right wing" of the church. Jesus, he declared, had been hijacked by the religious right. "Love is practice, not piety," Moyers said. "I have heard it asked: Who gave us authority to change the meaning of the Church? How did we let creed override compassion?" (Let's Get Jesus Back," Bill Moyers, *The United Methodist Reporter*, April 8, 2005, pp. 4a-5a). As I read his comments, I knew that I needed to hear and respond to his challenge to follow the prophetic, justice aspects of Jesus. Knowing myself to be a sinner, I know I can shrink Jesus down to my mold. Without realizing it, we who seek to evangelize the world can be blind to how compromised we have allowed biblical standards of purity and compassion to become. This self-understanding is a part of what has kept me in a pluralistic denomination, though I know there may be limits beyond which I cannot continue. I also knew as I read Moyers words that these were old charges of the left against the right, freshened by the current politics of the day. I find in such attacks an imbalance, a reduction of Jesus that reflects the kind of limitation of viewpoint it seeks to critique.

When Jesus took the bread and the cup and said, "Do this in remembrance of me," he was calling us to a pietistic act that provides a creedal foundation and spiritual resources for the practice of similar acts of love. The Jesus whom Bill Moyers wants to get back has legitimacy; he is the Jesus whose sufferings Paul wants to share. But what about the power of the Resurrection? Knowing Jesus is not a matter of either piety or practice, but of both. Most of us lean one way or the other, and as sinners who like to spin things to suit us, we need help to know more of Jesus.

And if on some point you think differently,
that too God will make clear to you

Jesus, in the spirit of the prophets, "spoke truth to power." This is sometimes the role of the church as it stands with the "least of these." The rise of the so-called right wing in this last generation was, in part, a reaction to the unwillingness of socially prophetic voices in the church to affirm the evangelical distinctives of the New Testament. There was a strongly felt need to speak that truth to the power of academia, which has replaced the evangel with a secular message of equality among religions and an evolutionary view of moral standards. Theology schools and universities often exist side by side. Who has converted whom? When will the left wing of the spectrum face its capitulation to secular redefinitions of salvation, love and toleration?

What an awesome and continually challenging thing it is to want to know him, the power of his resurrection and the fellowship of his sufferings!

Obedience: A Way to Real Knowledge

becoming like him in his death

Like the Trinity itself, this trinity of knowing, i.e., knowing Jesus, the power of his resurrection and the fellowship of his sufferings, is not a collection of separate entities. It is an interwoven whole, a diamond with many facets. Knowing the power of his resurrection can imply many possibilities, particularly those associated with justification by faith and baptism in the Holy Spirit. Continuing with the image of growing in our knowledge of Jesus Christ as we respond to his knocking, a dynamic way we come to know this power is in responding to the call to obedience.

Experience teaches us that it is usually only as we seek to be obedient that we recognize our need for this power. Otherwise, it is a luxury. But beyond this, the Christ hymn (2:5-11) reveals that even in the life of Jesus, it was obedience that released the Father to respond in power to the Son, to exalt him. Hebrews 6 tells us that without faith it is impossible to please God. Biblical faith always includes obedience, which means action. That is why when we hear Jesus knocking, and allow him into our hearts and minds to know him better, it is not long before we hear him knocking from without, calling us back into the world to live out our faith and apply our knowledge.

John 7:17 reads, "If anyone chooses to do God's will, he will find out whether my teaching comes from God or whether I speak on my own." In other words, if we want to know just how authoritative Jesus Christ is, we must walk in obedient faith. Then we will grow in knowledge and in his grace. Augustine commented, "Understanding is the reward of faith . . . . What is 'If any man be willing to do his will?' It is the same thing as to believe."

Dick Wills, now a United Methodist bishop, as a pastor discovered the power of the Resurrection to raise a traditional congregation to new life. His story, told in *Waking to God's Dream*, contains elements common to many pastors' stories. In the years after seminary he found the idea of a *career* replaced his idea of *calling*. His ministry, successful by most denominational measurements, was like Calliet's book, something of his own making. The making of it had led him to burnout. A journey to South Africa opened his eyes to spiritual resources for which he had been substituting his own strenuous efforts. Upon returning home he determined that he was going to shift paradigms and engage the power of God in the laity.

Central to such a resurrection is this principle (#2 of eight principles found in *Waking to God's Dream*): God blesses obedience. Dick Wills affirms that principle repeatedly to the people he serves. This is not an obedience rooted in fear of God. It is founded upon gratitude for God's gift of hope in our hopelessness. Taking it seriously has released the power of the Resurrection.

Wills is quick to note that even though obedience will ultimately lead to blessing, it may first lead to misunderstanding and/or rejection. He relates a painful example in his experience of what are sometimes referred to as the "worship wars." In seeking to be obedient, his church expanded their worship offerings to Friday and Saturday night, as well as shifting worship experiences around on Sunday morning. A man Dick counted as a friend, a person whom he appreciated and respected, came to him with the news that his family was leaving the church. He did not like the new music at the 9:30 service. Dick pointed out that the music this man preferred was used at the 11:00 service and encouraged him simply to move to that service. In response, the man informed him that he had a regular golf tee off time of 12:00 noon. Dick replied, "If it meant that with this new kind of music we could reach people who are hurting and living in great darkness and brokenness and share with them the love of Jesus, would you be willing to shift your tee time 15 minutes to 12:15?" The reply was simple and direct, "Hell, no!" (p. 67)

This was not the kind of price martyrs pay for obedience, but it is more like the kind most of us might have to pay. Dick shares the story, not to condemn the man, but to illustrate that obedience has its price.

While various Christians might disagree as to how God's power is manifested, at its root is the obedience of faith. Paul longed to know such blessed, costly obedience as part of the journey toward knowing the One whose obedience opened doors to resurrection power.

Tom Landry, coach of the Dallas Cowboys football team for the better part of 30 years said, "The job of a football coach is to make men do what they don't want to do in order to achieve what they've always wanted to be" (quoted in *Spiritual Disciplines for the Christian Life*, Donald Whitney, p. 20). This is the call of Jesus, the call to lose one's life in order to find it.

To Know Jesus Is to Know Suffering

and the fellowship of his sufferings

Paul affirms this principle as he declares his desire to know the fellowship of Christ's sufferings. With the benefit of a long look back, I realize that James and John were profoundly naive when they expressed a willingness to drink the cup that Jesus would drink. Even so, in my gut I am still very close to Peter who knew Jesus enough to proclaim, "You are the Christ, the Son of the living God," yet shortly thereafter rebuked Jesus for his talk of suffering and death (Matthew 16: 15ff.). This is the way, as Jesus put it, "men think." Somewhere in the journey of faith in Jesus Christ a corner must be turned, where a believer quits being dominated by the way "men think." In God's love, as in all love, there is inevitable suffering because of the needs of those who are loved. How many ways are there for God to suffer? How many people, at just this moment in history, could be classified as "the least of these" with whom Jesus directly identifies?

Some years ago I ran across a story entitled "The Cockpit." One of the characters of that story says to the other that he marvels when he thinks of the peace of God. The other replies that it is not the peace of God that amazes her, but the pain of God. In Psalm 51 we read, "Against you and you only have I sinned and done that which is evil in your sight." When I hear those words, I am reminded that all the variations of sin—all the embarrassment, inconvenience, shame, heartbreak, agony, frustration, loss of hope, fear, failure, hunger, deprivation, all of the pain—finally come home to the heart of God against whom all sin is ultimately committed.

An old rabbi is said to have asked a faithful student, "Do you love me?" The student replied, "You know that I do." The rabbi responded, "Then do you know what causes me pain?" "No." "If you are not close enough to know what causes me pain, then you are not close enough to love me."

This is why Paul wants to share the sufferings of Jesus. It is not some kind of born-again masochism. It is a longing to have the capacity to return some of the love that flows out of Jesus. That love is the most real, the most solid thing in the cosmos. Paul will be satisfied with nothing less. When we seek to obey the Great Commandment to love God with all that we are, we discover how disabled sin has made us, how much we need the life-giving, death-overcoming power of the Resurrection. Our attempts at obedience magnify the depths of our need for grace. They also magnify the depths of the love that has reached out for us "while we were yet sinners." "Love so amazing, so divine," as Charles Wesley put it, demands our all. Even more, it bids us taste that love and the suffering that inevitably accompanies it. I recall an advertisement for a ministry that reached out to the hurting in the world. Its headline read, "Let my heart break with the things that break the heart of God." Somehow even knowing that pain, fearsome as it might be, brings life. To know it in fellowship with Jesus Christ, is to know at the same time the love of God. No wonder Jesus, speaking of Paul, had told Ananias, "I will show him how much he must suffer for my name" (Acts 9:16).

One of the sweet experiences of my life took place watching my oldest daughter on stage in a college production of A *Shayna Maidel* by Barbara LeBow. This was the story of a Jewish family, a father, mother and two daughters. In the 1920s the father and one daughter leave Germany and come to the United States. Due to illness, the mother and other daughter remain behind. Late in the play it is revealed that the father's financial stinginess had delayed the departure of his wife and daughter waiting in Germany. Then the Depression hit and eventually the mother and daughter, still in Germany, end up in a concentration camp.

As the play begins the daughter who had come to the States, Rose, has become a young woman. She is enjoying life in New York City. Then her father informs her that the sister who was left behind will soon be arriving and is expecting to live with Rose. When Lucia, the sister, arrives, the tension begins. The contrast between the two is stark. Lucia's clothes are literally rags. She speaks little English. A number has been tattooed on her arm. The gulf between them seems insurmountable.

Two moments in the play are especially dramatic. The first is a reading of the list of the names of their extended family and Lucia's response to each name, usually "murdered at Auschwitz," etc. What if those were the names of my family? It was a powerfully searching encounter with the pain of those years. The second wrenching moment comes as Rose sees pictures of her mother, a mother she could not remember and would never know. When Rose is left alone she cries out for her mother and then, taking a pen, firmly writes a number on her own arm. She had entered into the fellowship of the suffering of her family.

That was all moving enough, but what followed was icing on the cake. The director had taken the cast, as part of their preparation, to meet a Jewish couple who had survived the Holocaust. This couple had attended the first performance and a simple reception was held in their honor afterward. The husband asked to speak. At a well-known Christian college, an evangelical institution, he said, "We feel that you are with us in what we have experienced. You have shared our pain." My wife, standing next to me, had exactly the same thought I did. She leaned over and whispered, "The fellowship of his sufferings." In that moment I sensed Paul's longing to hear the words, "You have shared my pain," from the Lord.

That wonderful Jewish couple would have had every right to lash out at this group of comfortable young Christians. They could have said, "Who do you think you are to pretend that you even begin to grasp the nightmare, the grief of our lives!" But with utmost grace they opened their hearts and their pain and gave that group the highest privilege they could give—the fellowship of their sufferings.

Only let us live up to what we have already obtained.

In Matthew 7 Jesus sternly warns against those for whom their faith is either only talk or only power. To such he will say, "I never knew you." My guess is that such people never knew him, never knew the fellowship of his pain, never got in touch enough with their own pain to let Jesus into the labyrinth of their sin and sorrow. Paul lived with no such denial or illusions. His need was clear. It led him to long for the ultimate remedy: the saving, pain-filled love of God in Jesus Christ. There would be no half-way attempt. He wanted to know and be known. How much of Jesus do you and I want to know?

Questions for Discussion

1. How are love and suffering related? How does faith in Jesus make suffering a positive part of life?

2. Re-read Philippians 2:5-11. What does it tell us about knowing God?

3. What is the difference between knowledge "about God" and knowledge "of God"?

4. Why can "experience" be such a powerful competitor to scripture as the source of authority?

5. "To be born again means that I see Jesus." When Calliet saw Jesus in the gospels it gave birth to a whole new view of God. Why does Jesus have such an impact?

6. John Wesley had to warn some Methodists not to depend on their experiences but to stay anchored in the Scriptures. Why would he have issued such a warning?

7. Why is obedience to God so crucial in the life of faith? Why can God bless obedience?

8. Does Dick Wills' experience with the man who left church sound familiar? What might it say about being "purpose driven"?

9. Is it possible to grow as a human being without giving up some freedom for the sake of a greater freedom? How is "losing our life" at the heart of discipline?

10. Why is it a blessing, a gift from God, to be able to share in God's sufferings?

CHAPTER ELEVEN

Standing Firm, but Not Still

Philippians 3:13b, 18, 19c, 4:1-2, 4-9

But one thing I do—Forgetting what is behind and straining toward what is ahead, I press on . . . .For, as I have often told you before and now say again even with tears, many live as enemies of the cross of Christ . . . Their mind is on earthly things . . .Therefore, my brothers, you whom I love and long for, my joy and crown, that is how you should stand firm in the Lord, dear friends! I plead with Euodia and I plead with Syntyche to agree with each other in the Lord . . . .Rejoice in the Lord always. I will say it again: Rejoice! Let your gentleness be evident to all. The Lord is near. Do not be anxious about anything, but in everything, by prayer and petition, with thanksgiving, present your requests to God. And the peace of God, which transcends all understanding, will guard your hearts and your minds in Christ Jesus. Finally, brothers, whatever is true, whatever is noble, whatever is right, whatever is pure, whatever is lovely, whatever is admirable—if anything is excellent or praiseworthy— think about such things. Whatever you have learned or received or heard from me, or seen in me—put it into practice. And the God of peace will be with you.

In this next part of Philippians Paul delivers a string of exhortations that have as their heart the deeply felt words of 4:1, "Therefore, my brothers, you whom I love and long for, my joy and crown, that is how you should stand firm in the Lord, dear friends."

The challenge to stand firm is typical of Paul. In Ephesians he borrows an everyday sight to illustrate this posture, " . . . put on the full armor of God, so that when the day of evil comes, you may be able to stand your ground, and after you have done everything, to stand. Stand firm then . . ." (6:13,14a). Forget any kind of bunker mentality. Standing firm is not passive or stationary. Putting on the whole armor of God to stand firm in the faith implies preparation for proactive, vigorous engagement with life's battles. As this letter continues to unfold, Paul forcefully puts forth pastoral imperatives for standing firm in the fight while actively pressing on toward the goal to win the prize. This is still the aggressive gospel warrior who told us to work out our salvation. To stand in the faith does not mean to stand still.

To Guard the Fruits, Tend the Roots

A pastor does not have to go far to find "brothers" and "dear friends" who need help standing firm. I recall an afternoon of visiting that confirmed this. In one situation a husband was dealing with the loss of his wife; in another a retired type-A professional was adjusting to impaired mobility due to multiple physical problems. As if these were not tough enough, in the third I encountered Job. The difficulties in the final home appeared to the casual observer to be associated with various health problems. In reality they involved violent family conflicts about which no one in the community knew. I experienced what Paul felt for the Philippians, an almost desperate wish that they would face their challenges fully engaged with Jesus. I wanted them to "do everything" they could do to stand. That's what this section of Philippians is about—doing everything we can do to live in the flow of God's grace and truth.

Each of the lives I visited was in a storm, with winds stirring up all kinds of emotional and spiritual trash, from fear masquerading as a controlling attitude to a lack of gratitude. The same was true of the people in Philippi. Paul was concerned that the trash would take over. He sought to provide strong encouragement to stand firm in the faith against the polluting winds of the world, the flesh and the devil.

Peter Marshall, former chaplain of the U. S. Senate, in his sermon, "Keepers of the Springs," takes a page from the master teacher and addresses the essence of Paul's concern with a parabolic story. It's the simple tale of a mountain village that had experienced financial struggles. As an economy measure the town council eliminated a position called "keeper of the springs." It wasn't a controversial move. Most people didn't know there was such a job. The keeper of the springs did his work unseen by others. All through the year he made his way up and down the mountains that surrounded the village, checking on the sources of water. As the seasons ran their courses, it was common for leaves, silt, creatures who live in the water and even dead animals to clog small creeks and springs located up in the hills. From day to day he kept such debris from blocking the flow of the water or affecting its purity.

At first the lack of his services went unnoticed. But then unexplained problems developed. Sickness became increasingly common. Coincidentally, a brown tint and noticeable odor signaled that something fundamental had changed in their water supply. At last someone had the presence of mind to put the pieces together. The unseen, distant springs had suffered from lack of regular maintenance. What had been thought a luxury was discovered to be a necessity. Action was taken to reinstate the position of keeper of the springs. In a few weeks there was a definite change for the better. The water cleared up and sickness declined. Citizens learned a lesson.

Peter Marshall had home and family in mind, thinking specifically of mothers as the essential keepers of life's developmental springs. Here in the letter to the Philippian believers, Paul acts as a "keeper of the springs" in the developing early church. By so doing he is very much in harmony with the burden of the Old Testament prophets captured in Jeremiah's message from God: "My people have committed two sins; They have forsaken me, the spring of living water, and have dug their own cisterns, broken cisterns that cannot hold water" (2:13). To stand firm, believers must carefully tend the basic sources of their God-given life.

Digging our own inadequate cisterns, possibly of the intellect or the pocketbook or the social scene or the success/power position, permits an easy forsaking of the springs of living water. So Paul simultaneously seeks to keep the springs of grace clear and flowing while identifying broken cisterns to which believers can easily return. Asbury Seminary's professor of preaching Dr. Charles Killian used jokingly to quote his mother, who reportedly opined, "You can lead a horse to water, but if you can get it in there and floating on its back you've got something!" The apostle was encouraging these disciples-in-the-making to continue their repentance, their turning from old cisterns and from attitudes and actions that clog the springs of living water in their lives. At the same time he knew that the best defense is a good offense, and he leads them to drink of what is excellent and praiseworthy.

Don't Forget to Forget

> *But one thing I do: Forgetting what is behind,*
> *and straining toward what is ahead, I press on to take hold*
> *of that for which Christ Jesus took hold of me.*

One of the foremost clogger-uppers of the springs of life in Christ is an unhealthy relationship with our past. Paul was concerned enough about this danger to write, ". . . one thing I do: Forgetting what is past, and straining toward what is ahead, I press on . . . ." (3:13b-14a). He overstates his actions to make a point. Our past can act as a signpost, but it should not become a hitching post.

In the last few days I have spent time getting acquainted with a man who could serve as the poster person for addictive behaviors. Approaching mid-life, he has been through rehab several times, always relapsing into drugs and alcohol. As I listened and responded, I was struck again with what a fundamental role lies play in clogging up a life of addiction. For example, he told how he had stayed clean and sober for more than a year, and then one day gave in to the offer of a drink. His reasoning was, "Hey, I quit before; I can quit again." This is a person who needs to turn from old lies and "forget" his past. That is, he needs to stop seeing himself as a person who can allow alcohol in his life. That old self must be "forgotten" as an option.

Of course, this is much easier to say than do. That is why Paul does not encourage such forgetting as a unilateral act. It must be done in tandem with "remembering" a new future: "I press on toward the goal to win the prize for which God has called me heavenward in Christ Jesus (3:14)." I recall hearing Paul Mickey, then a professor at Duke Divinity School, say, "To forgive is not to forget. It is to remember in a new way." This is how Christians keep the past from clogging up the present. We remember it in a new way.

We remember it as a person who has received a pardon remembers his crime. We remember it the way a person who has been adopted remembers his former longing for a family. We remember it the way a patient remembers his life before the cancer was removed.

This man who felt so defeated in his addictions kept repeating, "I wish I could believe I was forgiven." This was a lie that was clogging up the spring of grace. The truth was that he wished he could quit feeling so bad about being a failure.

When we have trouble "forgetting" the past because we are struggling to forgive someone else, it is obvious we do not want to relinquish the feeling of control it gives us to hold a grudge. This is giving in to a lie. We are anything but in control, but it is still a common sort of denial and a major clog producer.

When we have trouble forgetting the past, as did this man, because we find it hard to believe we are forgiven, the same trash is clogging up the springs. Accepting forgiveness is an act of surrender, of humiliation, of giving up spring-clogging control. It's as though life was a great equation. If we forsake God on one side, the springs of life clog up on the other. If we forsake the fleshly self on one side, the springs of life begin to flow on the other. Twelve-step programs work because they can help us do the right kind of forsaking for the right reasons. In so doing, they illustrate the effort needed simply to stand in some semblance of control of one's life ("having done all, to stand").

I related to this struggling pilgrim the old story of the person who told his priest that he just could not believe that God could forgive *his* sins. He was a special case. The priest replied, "Go into the sanctuary and stand before the large crucifix there. Look up at Jesus and tell him, "I'm sorry. It just isn't enough for my sins." That is a humbling position to be in, but God can use it to help us do the right kind of forsaking, the forsaking of self-righteousness. The unconscious desire to determine what God can and cannot forgive withers when it truly witnesses what happened on the Cross, releasing the springs of living water to strengthen and refresh.

No, the past is seldom truly forgotten, but the drive to be in control that led to rebellion in the past should never be remembered in the same way after we have put the past into Jesus' crucified hands. This is why in Philippians 3:16 Paul says, "Only let us live up to what we have already attained." That is, let's allow what is past to remain "disempowered" by the Cross and paled by the high calling toward which we now stretch our hands. To paraphrase missionary martyr Jim Elliot, "he is no fool who forsakes what only clogs up life in order to receive the living water which alone gives life."

agree with each other in the Lord

A man in one place I served was known as one of those people "born in the objective case." You could count on him to have a complaint and to register it strongly. He was a commanding personality with whom no one wanted to tangle. As my time in that congregation stretched into years, he began to comment on things in sermons that were speaking to him. I was glad to hear such responses, but being the tough person he was, I did not expect any kind of transforming to take place.

Then one Sunday after worship, he came up to the front of the sanctuary and reminded me of an illustration I had used a few weeks earlier in addressing the need to put the past behind us. "This week," he calmly announced, "I went to a man who did me wrong 20 years ago and got right with him. There is another man with whom I must do the same thing. I will see him soon." Few things in my ministry have blessed me more.

Recently, he asked if I had the address of a former pastor. I knew some of the story and why he wanted that address. That week I found the address and called his house. His wife answered. When she told me he was not there, I asked if she would write down the address her husband had requested. "Oh, no!" she responded. "I wonder why he wants that!" But I was not worried. I knew he wanted to "forget" something in the Lord and to forsake the right things. I rejoiced. While this man could be a formidable presence, I knew Christ was in him, wanting to spring up with life.

Don't Forget to Remember

their mind is on earthly things

It is easy to read over the words that come next (3:17ff.) and fail to be gripped by the depth of feeling behind them. Paul speaks of his tears (vs.18) at the very thought that "many live as enemies of the cross of Christ." He goes on to describe those who routinely sell their spiritual birthright (who forsake the wrong thing) for a mess of pottage, the satisfaction of the moment. Again, his remedy for this giant clog is not "just say 'No.'" It is a profoundly rich awareness that we were created for more significant things, an eternal relationship with God that fundamentally alters the nature of who we ought to be in the here and now.

In any journey the destination determines how the trip is undertaken. While heaven might sound like pie in the sky by and by when you die, the knowledge that our destination is eternity with a God of holy love is immensely relevant now. It totally alters our identity, if we embrace it with all of our heart. "Everyone who has this hope in him purifies himself . . ." (I John 3:3).

Paul's status as both a Roman citizen and a part of the chosen people gave him two functional ways in which to understand how one's identity could reach beyond immediate circumstances.

Travel authority John Gunther told a story that illustrated how Eastern bloc communists in the Cold War days identified with "the party" beyond their immediate circumstances. A woman was seen walking down the street of a city in one of the satellite countries behind the Iron Curtain. Although it was a beautiful sunny day, she had opened her large umbrella and was walking along beneath it. When asked why she had hoisted the umbrella when there wasn't a cloud in the sky, she replied, with a snort, "In Moscow it is raining!" Her "citizenship" had moved beyond physical circumstances.

In 2 Corinthians 4 and 5 Paul speaks of what is temporary and what is lasting. In what sounds like an impossibility, he tells believers to fix their eyes on what cannot be seen. "For what is seen is temporary, but what is unseen is eternal"(4:18b). This is central to a life lived "by faith, not by sight"(5:7). He is saying as directly as possible that another major spring polluter is our identification with things directly accessible to our senses rather than with unseen but eternal realities. The communist woman had fixed her eyes on things unseen, on her beliefs and the bonds they created. That was more relevant than the weather around her.

The Lord is near

My father-in-law's parents used to send their five children off with the loving reminder, "Remember who you are and whose you are." They were protecting the springs of life by suggesting: "Remember that what is unseen, your identity as part of this Christian family, is more significant than what you can see—the pressure of your immediate circumstances."

We have a term for people who forget who they are and whose they are, who get off the main road and simply follow the side roads wherever they may lead: They are *lost*. Look around at modern and postmodern culture, even in the church, and what you often see are lost people desperately trying to convince the world that their side road is a main road. Or if they cannot do that, then declaring that there is no main road. Paul strongly affirms that there is a main road, and that it is the road of the high calling of God in Jesus Christ that leads us heavenward. It cannot be seen with the eye, but it is far more real than anything physical sight can perceive. It is like the North Star by which we can always reckon our position regardless of the changes in our immediate situation. "The world and its desires pass away, but the man who does the will of God lives forever" (1 John 2:17).

George Matheson, who wrote the beautiful hymn, "O Love That Wilt Not Let Me Go," was a poet and a preacher. He was also blind. One day a woman who attended the church where George Matheson preached was seen moving out of her basement apartment up several flights to another apartment in the same building. When asked why she was going to the trouble of moving within the same building, she answered, "You just can't listen to George Matheson preach and live in a basement." George Matheson did not need physical eyes to see what is truly real, nor to show it to others in a compelling way.

Nothing Works on Tough Clogs Like Humility

The next admonition we encounter involves two women in the Philippian congregation, Euodia and Syntyche. These are people Paul knew well. It is noteworthy that Paul, often stereotyped as a male chauvinist, speaks of these women as co-laborers for the cause of the gospel. In Acts 16, we learn that Paul's first contact in Philippi was a woman, Lydia, a successful seller of purple cloth. This was a church where women played a significant role.

There is also reference to a "loyal yokefellow" (4:3) for whom no further identification is offered. No hints are given as to the issue that divided these two women, nor who the person is whom Paul calls upon to take the role of peacemaker. All we can say is that it was a situation the apostle took seriously, one familiar to the whole church. Knowing that letters such as this were read before the entire congregation, Paul is obviously seeking to leverage the weight of the body against this interpersonal clog in the springs of healthful fellowship.

Let your gentleness be evident to all

That is why this matter was included in the letter—to affirm in a flesh-and-blood situation just how important it is for the church to seek to live in peace. Paul was not prone to sweep disagreements under the rug. When he told the proponents of circumcision in Galatia (the sort of people referred to in 3:2 of this letter as "dogs") that he wished they would simply go ahead and castrate themselves (5:12), he was not running from a fight. But near the end of that same letter he writes, "May I never boast except in the cross of our Lord Jesus Christ, through which the world has been crucified to me, and I to the world" (6:14). In other words, "Don't let your ego become the issue." Too many disagreements are actually squabbles over control. The pride that often drives such divisions clogs the channels of healthy relationships as fast as any debris known to humankind. Terry Tekyl, who ministers around the world on the subject of prayer, enjoins those who would fan the flames of church disputes, "Don't go to the phone, go to the throne!" There's a gospel chorus that says, "You can talk about me as much as you please, I'll talk about you while I'm on my knees." That's hokey, but it's also healthful. When I was in seminary, it used to be said about sermon preparation that a preacher ought to spend an hour in the study for every minute in the pulpit. Most pastors would consider that a luxury, but the math applies well in our response to disagreements with others in the church. An hour on our knees for every minute of "talk" would probably serve as an effective prophylactic against the debilitating effect of self-righteous toxins. Like Paul, I exaggerate to make the point. Those who have ears to hear, let them hear.

Higher Ground: God's Pest Control

Rejoice in the Lord always. I will say it again: Rejoice!

Philippians 4:4-9 are a half-dozen of the richest verses in the Bible. Several books could be generated from the thoughts of these verses alone. Together they are a powerful expression of what Paul had in mind in 2:12b-13 when he said, ". . . continue to work out your salvation with fear and trembling. For it is God who works in you to will and to act according to his good purpose." In Matthew 11:28f.), we read the Great Invitation of Jesus which invites us to come to him and find rest in his yoke. We are told that his yoke is easy and his burden is light. So how do we square this with the call to *work out* our salvation?

The Lord is near.

We accept the truth of 2:13 that God is at work in us and we realize, as Jesus said in John 15:5, "I am the vine; you are the branches. If a man remains in me and I in him, he will bear much fruit; apart from me you can do nothing." Yes, even our decisions to work out our salvation would be impossible apart from God's help. While we often say that we believe in free will, what we actually experience is free grace. The free grace of God enables us to have the precious gift of choice. Apart from him our only choice would be to sin.

This free grace is similar to those mountain springs in Peter Marshall's sermon. We don't see it. We take it for granted. As long as the springs are clean and open our lives are "easy." But they do not stay open naturally, and this is where the fundamental work of discipleship begins—keeping the springs open. We must constantly work at "coming unto Jesus." The most strategic work of the Christian faith is abiding in Christ. This means real time spent in the Word of God, in prayer, in worship, in responding to the inner nudges of the Spirit to obedience.

Few things can blast free the clogs of the springs of living water like earnest praise to the Lord. Here we encounter some of the best known words of this letter (4:6), "Rejoice in the Lord always. I will say it again: Rejoice!" Praise is a decision of the will that reflects a free flowing spring and also releases a clogged up spring. C. S. Lewis said, "Praise is inner health made audible." This inner health is the by-product of choosing to look beyond oneself, the effects of which are magnified by focusing on the source of life himself. The decision to rejoice, even if it does not feel natural—even if it is a "sacrifice,"—takes "me" out of the center. This in turn helps release God's power. The link between praise and spiritual health was affirmed by Bishop Fulton Sheen when he wrote, "The power of rejoicing is always a fair test of a man's moral condition."

Dr. J.C. McPheeters was a spiritual giant whose life was a commentary on the power of rejoicing. He was the kind of person who changed the atmosphere in a room for the better simply by walking into it. In the later years of his life, having outlived his wife, he moved into one of the men's dormitories at Asbury Theological Seminary, where he had served as president. Every morning before the sun came up, students closest to his room could hear his feet hit the floor and his booming voice declare, "This is the day that the Lord hath made. I will rejoice and be glad in it!" At Dr. McPheeter's funeral, David Seamands spoke of the powerful positive influence of this servant of God. In an image that I will always remember, he said that Dr. McPheeters lived high up on the mountain where snakes cannot survive. That's what rejoicing does, it takes us up on the mountain where snakes don't go. Praising God is the best preventative maintenance a Christian can perform.

Do not be anxious about anything, but in everything, by prayer and petition, with thanksgiving, present your requests to God

Having strongly called for a spirit of rejoicing, Paul continues, encouraging a gentle spirit and reminding his readers of the nearness of him who said, "I am with you always." Then he points the church to the heartbeat of a life of faith, thankful prayer (4:6). Like praise, thanksgiving can remove the handcuffs of self-absorption that so easily shackle every human life. This, he affirms, has the power to release the flow of God's peace, which, in turn, protects our hearts and minds from the ravages of a self-centered existence.

I spoke earlier of my father-in-law's family. Rural South Georgia in the Depression years was not an area of abundance, unless you enjoyed sand gnats. Yet his humble home was blessed by the Lordship of Jesus Christ. The father of this family, Morris Key, would often say, "We are so rich!" He meant it, and his children understood his words. When Morris Key died before his wife, Bertha, she gathered the five children around her by the casket and said, "We have so much to be thankful for." While their grief was very real, the snakes of self-pity and doubt could not survive on the mountain of gratitude to the Lord. The springs of living water flowed even in the desert of sorrow.

Keep the Stink out of What You Think: Abide in Jesus

think about such things

Paul's next exhortation is one of the most challenging in the Scriptures: whatever is true, noble, right, pure, lovely, admirable, excellent, praiseworthy—think about such things (4:8). It should be noted that he does not say, "Think *only* about these things." Neither Paul nor the prophets could be held to such a monastic kind of standard. Still, the call to nobility of focus is clear and unapologetic.

One does not have to be a follower of Jesus to appreciate the overwhelming need for this kind of mental protection in the 21st century. Prior to Lot pitching his tent near Sodom where the men "were wicked and were sinning greatly against the LORD" (Genesis 13:13), persons of faith have had to work at keeping the springs of righteousness unobstructed. Imagine what those folks in Sodom would have done in today's sensate world. That's right, exactly the same things we are doing. Sin is not original, but it is predictable. Therefore, we must be predictable in our response to sin in ourselves. Galatians 5:24-25 says, "Those who belong to Christ Jesus have crucified the sinful nature [with] its passions and desires. Since we live by the Spirit, let us also keep in step with the Spirit." As was mentioned earlier, we "forget" the past, both the deeds for which we have sought forgiveness, and the fleshly control that precipitated those deeds. When these things rear their heads again, as they will, we remember them in a new way. They are part of what we now recognize as a dysfunctional pattern of life (the way/law of sin and death). The wages of that pattern of life is what Jesus paid on the cross. His death and resurrection are the quintessence of what is true, noble, right, pure, lovely, admirable, excellent and praiseworthy. Anything that contradicts this influence must be discarded.

At the same time, we must fortify ourselves by keeping in step with the Spirit, "thinking on" the things that make for true righteousness and peace. I wonder if Paul might have been thinking unconsciously, if not consciously, about the beautiful expressions of joy in the nobility of God's truth found in Psalms 19 and 119. Psalm 19:7ff. affirms the glory of God's ways with these lovely words:

> The law of the LORD is perfect, reviving the soul. The statutes of the LORD are trustworthy, making wise the simple. The precepts of the LORD are right, giving joy to the heart. The commands of the LORD are radiant, giving light to the eyes. The fear of the LORD is pure, enduring forever. The ordinances of the LORD are sure and altogether righteous. They are more precious than gold, than much pure gold;

they are sweeter than honey from the comb.
By them is your servant warned;
in keeping them there is great reward.

Psalm 119 makes this more personal, noting the blessings that come to those who seek God with all their hearts. "I have hidden your word in my heart that I might not sin against you" (119:11). Acknowledging the piety that these words reveal, we must pause to ask what, if anything, is different about Paul's thoughts in Philippians 4 from these rich expressions of truth and spiritual longing.

that is how you should stand firm in the Lord, dear friends

For the answer we go back to Philippians 4:1, the heart of this portion of the letter. Here Paul enjoins the Philippians to stand firm *in the Lord*. It would be easy to read this call to a noble mind-set and hop right back on the old covenant treadmill of trying harder. The examples of Psalms 19 and 119 illustrate the beauty and depth of what can be found there to challenge an earnest soul. But since those words were written, a miraculous event has occurred. God has provided a new spring of grace and truth, and it is available to whoever chooses to draw the strength to live on a higher plain.

This is what Paul was declaring in Romans 7 and 8 where he confesses his failure to live up to such high standards. "What a wretched man I am! Who will rescue me from this body of death? Thanks be to God—through Jesus Christ our Lord" (7:24-25a). Then in chapter eight he directly speaks of the importance of our minds in saying, "Those who live according to the sinful nature have their minds set on what that nature desires; but those who live in accordance with the Spirit have their minds set on what the Spirit desires. The mind of sinful man is death, but the mind controlled by the Spirit is life and peace . . . ." (8:5-6). And what does the mind controlled by the Spirit look like? We go back to

Philippians 2:5 where we read, "Your attitude should be the same as that of Christ Jesus . . . ." That attitude was one of utter surrender to and reliance upon the Father.

This means that our first job as seekers and believers is continually to drink from this new spring. The call to think about high things is part of what Paul had in mind in 2 Corinthians 10:5, ". . . we take captive every thought to make it obedient to Christ." Being under grace and not law means we always have one starting point for every line of thinking, Jesus and his grace. Holocaust survivor and author Corrie ten Boom used to say, "Don't wrestle, just nestle." In other words, the secret of our lives is not how hard we try but where we begin. We must nestle, abiding in Jesus Christ.

Wanted: Heavy Drinkers

put it into practice

When Paul then says, "Whatever you have learned or received or heard from me, or seen in me—put it into practice. And the God of peace will be with you" (4:9), he is not bragging about himself. His example is not one of magnificent wrestling with the law of God, but one of surrendered nestling in the grace of God through his Son.

In *Life on the Mississippi*, Mark Twain wrote, "Two things seemed pretty apparent to me. One was, that in order to be a [Mississippi River] pilot a man had got to learn more than any one man ought to be allowed to know; and the other was, that he must learn it all over again in a different way every 24 hours" (quoted by Warren Bennis in *On Becoming a Leader*, p. 101). Learning to stand, learning to do all that one can do with the help of God's grace, figuring out how to wear the whole armor of God without living a defensive life, being careful to tend the true springs of abundant living, all of this sometimes seems like more than any one person ought to have to know. And then in every stage of life these things have to be learned all over again. What makes it possible is the same thing that makes a river pilot's life possible—the continuous flow of water, in the case of a believer, of living water. As John R. W. Stott put it, Christians are spiritual dipsomaniacs, always drinking of the water of life. It is no coincidence that the final chapter of the Bible is about the river of life, including this invitation: "The Spirit and the bride say, 'Come!' And let him who hears say 'Come!' Whoever is thirsty, let him come, and whoever wishes, let him take the free gift of the water of life" (Rev. 22:17).

God has created the heart to function as a spring through which his living water can flow. The parable of the Prodigal Son was Jesus' way of affirming that the Father is the wellspring of grace. Whether or not we leave home, there must come a time when we realize this, empty our hands of shallow passion and pride and stretch out our hands in repentance and trust. Having done that, we then choose each day to leave the past behind and stay close to the spring from whence our true life flows.

What have you done this day, this week, to be sure you are drinking from those springs? Is there anything more important?

Questions for Discussion

1. What "springs" might need regular attention in a healthy life of Christian discipleship?

2. If it is true that we don't hold grudges, but rather that grudges hold us, why do we let such imprisonment go on? What has helped you let go of such grudges?

3. What does Paul mean by "the unseen," and how do we "fix our eyes" on it?

4. It has been said that the second most contagious thing in life is optimism and the most contagious thing is the lack of it. What

does this say about the importance of making peace in the church and the ease with which peace can be destroyed?

5. Have you ever dealt with control issues by praying for those who disagree with you? Did it make any difference? Did you change? Did they change?

6. Why is praise a sign of inner health?

7. What "snakes" does rejoicing in the Lord remove?

8. How can Paul's direction in these verses transform "stinking thinking"?

9. What regular practices/disciplines in your life enable you to drink the living water?

10. Is there anything you need to change to be sure that the springs of living water are open and flowing?

Hands Outstretched To Get In Sync With Jesus' Agenda
(The PERSON-Driven Life)

Philippians 4:10-19
I rejoice greatly in the Lord that at last you have renewed your concern for me. . . . I am not saying this because I am in need, for I have learned to be content whatever the circumstances.

I know what it is to be in need, and I know what it is to have plenty. I have learned the secret of being content in any and every situation . . . . I can do everything through him who gives me strength. Yet it was good of you to share in my troubles. . . . Not that I am looking for a gift, but I am looking for what may be credited to your account. . . . And my God will meet all your needs according to his glorious riches in Christ Jesus.

One of my favorite expressions is, "It's like my Grandmother's new false teeth. It just comes out in the conversation." This refers to the involuntary insertion of subject matter in everyday conversation.

For example, a grandparent compulsively refers to his new grandchild.

An anxious mother mentions her eligible daughter to single men.

The hypochondriac carefully explains his latest "condition."

In my part of the world, a true-blue University of Georgia fan feels it a religious duty to declare, "How 'bout them 'Dogs'!" It simply comes out in the conversation.

Paul also harbored a sacred compulsion. No matter what the subject, he always managed to turn toward Jesus Christ. We note this magnificent obsession in 1 Corinthians 2:2, ". . . I resolved to know nothing while I was with you except Jesus Christ and him crucified." One Sunday morning two young boys were seated on the steps of the chancel during the children's sermon. The pastor asked, "What's green, hops around and says, 'ribbit, ribbit'?" One boy turned to the other and said, "It sounds like a frog, but I know the answer is 'Jesus.'" Paul was equally predictable when it came to the Name above every name.

How the Man Who Really Has Everything Says "Thank You"

Yet it was good of you to share in my troubles . . . .
Not that I am looking for a gift

In the concluding verses of Philippians we encounter some of the New Testament's most quoted faith affirmations. These beloved scriptures are part of a rather awkward *Thank You* note that never uses the word *thanks*. Commentators have found Paul's stoic-sounding gratitude surprisingly near to damning with faint praise. He essentially says, "Thanks for your gifts, even if I didn't need them." In the *Interpretation* volume on Philippians, Fred Craddock provides a thoughtful review of the possible meanings of these rather left-handed compliments, concluding with this instructive observation about Paul:

> He is defined neither by wealth nor poverty but by a contentment that transcends both and by a power in Christ which enables him to live in any circumstance. It is important for his friends to see their gift in this context. The man to whom they sent it was not pacing his cell inquiring of the guard every five minutes whether the mail had come.

Their relationship to that man was not based on gifts and it would not be broken by the lack of them. As long as that is understood, said Paul, "I rejoice in the Lord greatly that now at length you have revived your concern for me." "It was kind of you to share my trouble" (p. 78).

How would a person whose home had been wired with electricity explain his diminished enthusiasm at the kind offer of a candle?

British journalist Malcolm Muggeridge, sitting with Mother Teresa in a television studio where she had gone to be interviewed, experienced the awkwardness of holy ingratitude. During a commercial break he was overcome by the irony of the moment as they watched an advertisement on a monitor. The product being promoted was a type of diet bread. Its primary virtue was that it had almost no food value. Declaring nothing more than the painfully obvious, Mother Teresa said something to the effect that it appeared Jesus was needed in television stations. How would she, having clearly seen the world through the eyes of Jesus, have said "thanks" for a loaf of non-nutritious bread?

When earlier in this letter Paul had declared, "For me to live is Christ," he was not creating fodder for future preachers. He was declaring a blessed fact. Formerly, like the prodigal's elder brother, he could not comprehend the idea of a Father who would abandon decorum, hike up his robe and run to meet the returning wastrel son. Now with his mind transformed, he understood that all are prodigals, some revealed more in sins of the flesh, others more in sins of the spirit, but all hopelessly in need of the Father's forgiving embrace. In that embrace Paul had received new eyes with which to see God's priorities. Paul had found a new definition of life in Christ Jesus.

I can do everything through him who gives me strength

Italian film director Roberto Rossellini attempted to capture the spirit of someone whose life was changed by Christ, Francis of Assisi. Rossellini's film, *Francis, God's Jester*, reenacts a scene from Francis' early spiritual journey as he encounters a leper while walking along a road. At first Francis is naturally repulsed, but eventually through Christ's guidance, Francis embraces the outcast, an experience likely unparalleled in the leper's years of disease. This spontaneous act of love foretells the powerful freedom from false security and power that Francis later experienced, a freedom issuing from the transformation of his mind due to the Lord's influence (Romans 12). Paul is just as radically changed and obviously as inspired to "work out" the implications of this new life.

Meeting Jesus—thinking Like Jesus

Following his encounter with Life on the Damascus Road, Paul initially became a fanatic, literally astonishing the believers who heard his witness. Acts 9:22 informs us, ". . . Saul grew more and more powerful and baffled the Jews living in Damascus by proving that Jesus is the Christ." He probably felt that *he* could do all things, including out-argue his Jewish opponents. In reality, this well-intentioned behavior proved to be effective anti-evangelism. His fleshly fervency was so overwhelming that the Jerusalem church finally had to ship him out of town in order for peace to return to their lives.

It was not that Paul needed more time to discover a new center for his life. That center was the same God he had always worshiped, who now had acted through Jesus of Nazareth to upend the entire spiritual order. "For God, who said, 'Let light shine out of darkness,' made his light shine in our hearts to give us the light of the knowledge of the glory of God in the face of Christ" (2 Corinthians 4:6). What Paul needed, and what most new believers need, is time to spiritually marinate, time to let light catch up with heat, time to mature spiritually. Dr. Ken Kinghorn, on the topic of the Holy Spirit, used to tell seminary students that self-control, the final item in the list of the fruit of the Spirit according to Paul, is usually the last virtue to "ripen" in a Christian's life. Could the apostle have been reflecting on his own life when he penned that list?

William Boggs has a bit of wisdom in the form of a conversation between a seeker and a saint:

The seeker asks, "Tell me please, wise one, how did you become holy?"

"Two words."

"And what are they, please?"

"Right choices."

"And how does one choose correctly?"

"One word."

"May I know it, please?"

"Growth."

"How does one grow?"

"Two words."

"What are those words, pray tell me?"

"Wrong choices" (*Sin Boldly: But Trust God More Boldly Still*, p. 48).

Do not be surprised if it takes time, perhaps years, to mature in your fruitfulness. Walking in the Spirit and having the mind that was in Christ Jesus are dimensions of Christian living that even St. Paul needed time to cultivate.

Jesus: New Lenses for Seeing God

When you have the freedom to "hug lepers," or in Paul's case, to hug Gentiles, something has definitely happened. 1 Samuel 10:6 says, "The Spirit of the LORD will come upon you in power . . . and you will be changed into a different person." Now writing to the Philippians from prison, an older but wiser believer, Paul wanted to reflect the fundamental difference it makes in everything to be "in Christ."

*And my God will meet all your needs according
to his glorious riches in Christ Jesus*

Paul's transformation, from the beginning, illustrates that
God's ways in Christ are not always compatible with traditional
paradigms. What we have here is a case of the conversion of an
initially unrepentant person. He was not seeking to change or
trying to change. Yet he changed! Why? How? The Holy Spirit
changed him! Why? Because at the heart of the gospel is *only the
call* to repent, to turn, to head in the direction of change. *Right
there with the call to turn in a new direction is the God who has
revealed himself in a new dimension.*

Craig Barnes, seminary professor and pastor, observed the
dynamics this creates, when he wrote, "Conversion always begins as
God's terrifying initiative in our lives. It scares us to think that God
would actually intervene in our good lives and say, 'I don't care how
devoutly you believe, you don't know who I am'. . . . No matter
how desperately we may want to change, we never will unless we
see God differently" *When God Interrupts*, p. 30). When we read the
words, "I can do all things through Christ who strengthens me,"
we are reading an invitation to the transformation of our minds
and the reorientation of our desires by direct contact with the light
of the knowledge of the glory of God in the face of Christ Jesus.
As Paul told the Romans, "Then [when the mind by transforming
grace begins to think like Jesus] you will be able to test and approve
what God's will is—his good, pleasing and perfect will" (12:2). If
such transformation is not part of a person's life, talk of being able
to do all things can easily digress into utter self-serving. Hence the
profound relevance of Paul's earlier injunction found in 2:5, "Let
this mind be in you, which was also in Christ Jesus" (KJV).

This underscores the significance of something Quaker
philosopher Elton Trueblood once expressed. As important as it is
to say that Jesus Christ is God, it may be more important that we
recognize that God is like Jesus Christ. When Paul spoke of Christ

he was not advocating some kind of unitarian, "ignore-the-Trinity-Jesus-is-all," theology. To the contrary, speaking of Jesus Christ always implied speaking of the Trinitarian God. Jesus is "the image of the invisible God…" (Colossians 1:15; 2 Corinthians 4:4). This same understanding is expressed in Hebrews 1:3, "The Son is the radiance of God's glory and the exact representation of his being, sustaining all things by his powerful word." What a difference it makes to realize that the mind of God and the mind of Jesus are alike in disposition. The mind of Christ, of course, is not limited to what we ordinarily think of as "the mind." Having the mind of Christ means obeying the Great Commandments to love God with all the heart, soul and mind, and one's neighbor as oneself (Matt. 22:37-39). It is a disposition of the heart and the will that alters our understanding of the place of power and control in our lives.

Making Peace with Weakness

I have learned the secret of being content in any and every situation, whether well fed or hungry, whether living in plenty or want

While the Bible is full of wonderful verses to help us seek this exchange of minds, few have been of more value on a daily basis to me than 2 Corinthians 12:10, which concludes, ". . . When I am weak, then I am strong." These words, "when I am weak, then I am strong," direct my mind to the life of Jesus, revealing the heart of God. I think of Philippians 2:6-11 where we are powerfully reminded of the voluntary weakness Jesus took upon himself. We are also reminded that in spite of voluntary weakness to the point of death, the power of God was not defeated. Rather, out of obedient weakness came eternal strength and victory. Those words change my understanding of God. They alter the appearance of weakness and apparent defeat. To say, "I can do everything through him who gives me strength," is not an arrogant or blindly idealistic affirmation. It is a declaration of *resurrection resilience*, which makes ultimate victory the default setting for those who, in their weakness, follow Jesus Christ.

During a difficult time in my ministry I felt I needed to absorb most of the stress being generated by those who opposed something I strongly supported. It resulted in a prolonged deep feeling of isolation. It was at that time I better understood the aloneness of Jesus as his mission unfolded. Literally no other person on the planet understood his mission, nor could one. My struggle lingered for several years, as it had for him.

What sustained me were the words of Jesus, which beyond all others have united my heart with strength, "I am with you always" (Matthew 28:20). In Jesus' prayer in John 17 He prays for believers in every age, asking, ". . . that all of them may be one, Father, just as you are in me and I am in you. May they also be in us so that the world may believe that you have sent me." Jesus could do all things through the Father who strengthened him. In like manner, our spiritual fruitfulness is predicated upon our abiding in the Strengthener. his mind and his strength are bound together.

Looking at the experiences of believers in the New Testament, we observe that doing all things speaks as much of endurance as deliverance. In *The Gospel According to Job* Mike Mason observes an interesting parallel between the ministry of Jesus and the post-Pentecost ministry of the apostles (pp. 365-66). In Jesus' ministry there seems to be a greater manifestation of supernatural power in the early months. As time passes, the apparently triumphant experiences begin to diminish and the cross moves inexorably onto center stage. Looking at the book of Acts we observe Paul as well as Peter miraculously liberated from prison cells early in their stories. As Paul grows older, he spends an increasing amount of time under some kind of arrest. In Acts 20 we read the moving scene of Paul's farewell to the Ephesian elders (which Mike Mason speaks of as a kind of parallel to the Last Supper and the beginning of "Paul's Passion"). Listen to Paul's words,

> And now, compelled by the Spirit, I am going to
> Jerusalem, not knowing what will happen to me there.
> I only know that in every city the Holy Spirit warns
> me that prison and hardships are facing me. However,
> I consider my life worth nothing to me, if only I may
> finish the race and complete the task the Lord Jesus has
> given—me the task of testifying to the gospel of God's
> grace (20:22-24).

It is obvious, isn't it, that saying "I can do all things" is not saying, "I can always do something obviously supernatural to make life easier" or "I can always get out of difficult circumstances." It is saying, as noted earlier, "I can do all things necessary to carry out the purpose for which Christ Jesus has taken hold of me."

Commenting on John 21:18, where Jesus warns Peter, "I tell you the truth, when you were younger you dressed yourself and went where you wanted; but when you are old you will stretch out your hands, and someone else will dress you and lead you where you do not want to go," Henri Nouwen makes this profound observation:

> The world says, "When you were young you were
> dependent and could not go where you wanted, but when
> you grow old you will be able to make your own decisions,
> go your own way, and control your own destiny." But
> Jesus has a different vision of maturity: It is the ability
> and willingness to be led where you would rather not go
> (*In the Name of Jesus*, p. 81).

This is a message many of us have not heard, but it reflects the life of Jesus and many who have followed him. The ability to do all things becomes all the more remarkable when we see it in this light.

Grasping True Greatness

When we read the temptation narrative in Matthew 4 we encounter the startling truth that Jesus is not interested literally in doing *all* things. It is also safe to say that he was not interested in taking up just any cross. The world is full of people who are taking up crosses, that is, making real sacrifices, for the sake of some kind of success—people working on PhDs, business people working 80-90 hours a week, parents who meet themselves coming and going so their children can be achievers. Such people may be making heroic sacrifices but not doing "all things" that Paul had in mind. Well known "success" author Stephen Covey observes,

> Many people with secondary greatness—that is social status, position, fame, wealth, or talent—lack primary greatness or goodness of character. You see, our love of ourselves will prompt us to take up crosses to succeed, that same love of self can quench true greatness. Jesus could have had all the secondary greatness he wanted, except for one thing: He loves you and me. And today, once again, he calls us to love Him and claim our true greatness (*Principle Centered Leadership*, p. 58).

In the recent past I conducted the funeral service of a 44 year old woman who died unexpectedly. She was the adopted daughter of a couple in the congregation I was serving. In her early adolescence, this young woman developed a life-controlling problem. Ultimately she was diagnosed as bipolar. Her adoptive parents faced what God faces, to one degree or another, with all of us—a child with a natural bent to self-destruct. They never gave up on her, in spite of great cost.

As with many others I have known who lived with alcoholics, long-term cancer patients, Alzheimer's victims, Down's Syndrome children and other chronic challenges, these parents found a way to do all things, some of the toughest things, through Christ who strengthened them. His mind, the mind of tough servanthood, led them to the Cross. His strength enabled them to do all things necessary to carry that burden.

In my remarks at her funeral, I noted two kinds of faith found in the juxtaposed Psalms of 22 and 23. While Psalm 23 refers to enemies and death, which make it a very meaningful expression of faith, it is the kind of faith that could fit nicely with what Stephen Covey termed "secondary greatness." Psalm 22, interestingly the most frequently quoted psalm in the New Testament, is another story. Its opening words, "My God, my God, why have you forsaken me?" begin with a perspective far different from that of still meadows and quiet waters. Immediately we are plunged into the "while-we-are-in-this-tent-we-groan-and-are-burdened" side of belief (2 Corinthians 5:4). Just three verses later in that same 2 Corinthians passage Paul writes, "We live by faith, not by sight." This is the character of Christian faith expressed elsewhere in some of Paul's most important words: *"For we know in part. . . ."* (1 Corinthians 13:9a) Indeed, a profoundly crucial element of Christian faith, a fundamental part of "all things" that can be accomplished through Jesus Christ, is to trust when no immediate or easy answer to our predicament can be seen. "For we know in part," yet by the grace of God the part that we do know includes Jesus Christ. Even when I ask, "Why?" I still "know *whom* I have believed" (2 Timothy 1:12).

Muhammad Ali, during his tempestuous years as a boxer, was on board a jet when the turbulence became strong and the captain of the airliner turned on the seatbelt light. Everyone in the airplane complied, except Ali. When the flight attendant pointed out his negligence, he replied in his typically audacious style, "Superman don't need no seatbelt!" The attendant didn't hesitate, when she said, "Superman don't need no airplane."

Faith in Christ does not mean we can do all things because we have suddenly become super human. The Christian faith takes advantage of the vine and branch relationship of which Jesus spoke in John 15. "I am the vine; you are the branches. If a man remains in me and I in him, he will bear much fruit; apart from me you can do nothing" (John 15:5). What Paul spoke of as "the law of the Spirit of life," an energy stronger than death, can flow into us and sustain us in all circumstances. And Paul points out the Cross as evidence of God's trustworthiness. "He who did not spare his own Son, but gave him up for us all—how will he not also, along with him, graciously give us all things?" (Romans 8:32)

Knowing Jesus—knowing Resurrection Life

according to his glorious riches in Christ Jesus

No wonder Paul told the Philippians, "I want to know Christ and the power of his resurrection and the fellowship of sharing in his sufferings, becoming like him in his death, and so, somehow, to attain to the resurrection from the dead" (3:10-11). There is no contradiction between the power of the resurrection and the reality of suffering. In point of fact, Paul clearly indicates that the two are inextricably woven together. Being able to do all things through Christ does not give us a "get-out-of-jail" pass from life's trials. It implies a relationship with Life Himself that is more enduring than all the "Why?" questions and all the struggles of life. Paul trustingly outstretched his hands to know Christ, and in so doing, to know how to overcome in that relationship.

Christian apologist Os Guinness described a prayer that became legendary in the Washington, D.C., area. Arthur Burns, who served presidents from Dwight D. Eisenhower to Ronald Reagan in such positions as chairman of the United States Federal Reserve System and ambassador to West Germany, was a man marked by *gravitas*. His wavy silver hair and signature pipe were part of a demeanor that fit his many high-level responsibilities.

Arthur Burns was Jewish. When he began attending an informal

White House prayer and fellowship group in the 1970s, he was accorded special respect. No one knew how to involve him in the group. Week after week when different people took turns ending the meeting in prayer Burns was passed over.

One week, however, the group was led by a newcomer who was not sensitive to this situation. As the meeting ended, the newcomer turned to Arthur Burns and asked him to close their time in prayer. Some of the old-timers glanced at one another, wondering what would happen. Without missing a beat, however, Burns reached out, held hands with others in the circle, and prayed this prayer, "Lord, I pray that you would bring Jews to know Jesus Christ. I pray that you would bring Muslims to know Jesus Christ. Finally, Lord, I pray that you would bring Christians to know Jesus Christ. Amen" (*The Call*, p. 106).

Knowing Jesus Christ opens doors of understanding and ability. In John 15 we hear Jesus say these words, "Apart from me you can do nothing." I do not know whether Paul was aware of those words, but they are the mirror image of "I can do everything through him who gives me strength." Neither is intended to be interpreted absolutely. Yet both come from the same understanding of the unique resources of a relationship of obedient faith with the risen Jesus.

Alex Haley, author of *Roots*, was strolling through the countryside one day when he came upon a surprising sight that was a study in possibilities. A large turtle was sitting on top of a fencepost. After viewing this unlikely situation, he walked over to the turtle and said, "One thing is for certain. You didn't get here by yourself." Paul lived in unceasing amazement at what God in Christ had done to enable helpless sinners (who could do nothing) to overcome the gravity of condemnation and death. To say that he could do all things through Christ who strengthened him was not to exaggerate or to brag. It was a statement of the obvious source of his new life, and that of the entire body of Christ. It was a Eucharistic affirmation, an act of thanksgiving.

While Paul's attitude in these verses is usually described as close to stoic, it is in his affirmation that he can do all things *through Christ*, which makes plain the nature of his boast. He would have offered a hearty "Amen" to Arthur Burns' prayer. Jesus is alive and one day every knee will bow in recognition of his strength to save. The power to do all things, the power that comes in knowing Christ, the power Paul clearly stated he wanted to know originated in the Resurrection. Just as he rejects all efforts at virtue which are not rooted in love, so he rejects all talk of power that is not grounded in Jesus' resurrection. British New Testament scholar N. T. Wright affirms the centrality of the Resurrection in the early church by observing, "Why did Christianity arise, and why did it take the shape it did? The early Christians themselves reply: We exist because of Jesus' resurrection. . . . There is no evidence for a form of early Christianity in which the Resurrection was not a central belief. Nor was this belief, as it were, bolted on to Christianity at the edge. It was the central driving force, informing the whole movement" (quoted in *Christianity Today*, April 23, 2001, p. 102, "Reflections"; from the book *The Challenge of Jesus*).

Do All Things with Thanksgiving

Paul's correspondence sails on a sea of humble gratitude for what God has accomplished through Christ Jesus. "I can do everything through him who gives me strength" is the other side of the faith coin from "The Lord is near. Do not be anxious about anything, but in everything, by prayer and petition, with *thanksgiving* [mine], present your requests to God. And the peace of God, which transcends all understanding, will guard your hearts and your minds in Christ Jesus" (4:56-7). Both are joyful statements of amazed gratitude.

Hebrews 12:2 calls us to fix our eyes on Jesus who endured the cross "for the joy set before him." That same verse speaks of Jesus as "the author and perfecter of our faith." Consider Jesus in the Upper Room, breaking the bread and lifting the cup, giving thanks for what they would one day represent! He was affirming, "I can do all things through the Father who strengthens me." In giving thanks well before Easter morning, Jesus was pioneering resurrection faith, anticipating the joy that the Father's faithfulness would give. In his trust of the Father, Jesus was already victorious, already doing all that was needed to overcome all things.

Yet it was good of you to share in my troubles.

Christian joy is obedient faith under the uplifting influence of thanksgiving.

To declare, as Paul does, "Rejoice in the Lord always. I will say it again: Rejoice!" (4:4) is to stretch out the hands of faith toward the risen Lord with thankful confidence that the will of God will not lead us where the power of God cannot enable us. I know this has the sound of a classic pious platitude. There have been times I have not *felt* that this is true. But I have also learned that in those times I have usually forsaken rejoicing in the Lord and replaced it with chewing on the cud of self-pity. These are often periods when I need to get with other believers and let their faith lift me. Remember the men who lowered their friend down through the roof for Jesus's healing touch (Mark 2)? There are portions of our faith journey when we must admit "apart from Jesus—in others—I can do nothing, not even rejoice." Doing all things through Christ sometimes demands the help of Christ in others. To ignore this reality is to live in the prison of pride.

As a pastor there have been situations and relationships in every congregation I have served that have brought me to the edge of a crisis of faith. Our first full-time church was an inner-city congregation, where we had five locks on the back door. There was not one day in that place that I felt anywhere close to strong. There were many days I felt despair.

Years later another appointment, as Methodists call them, pushed me to the edge of life's most frequent temptation—to quit. The old joke, applied to senior pastors, "Moses leaned on his staff and died," was partially coming to pass as I dealt with several interesting personalities.

Pastoral concerns limit what can be shared about such experiences, but I have learned the truth of the observation: Pastors are always either going into a crisis, in the midst of a crisis or coming out of a crisis.

Before I entered ministry, the first summer of marriage prior to beginning seminary, my wife and I were "Summer Youth and Children's Workers" in a mid-sized congregation in South Georgia. One evening we took a group of Junior High students out to "Lake Wilco." That was a mistake. Actually, the first mistake was not having scouted out Lake Wilco. One of the members of the congregation had a cabin at this lake and had offered it for our use, so we accepted the offer.

Lake Wilco turned out to be part of a swamp. It looked like snake-city. Had I lived in South Georgia before this, I would have been even more worried about alligators. It was one of those nights when the charcoal would not light. Once the fire got going (after singing every song we knew twelve times), the hamburger patties we bought were so fatty that they shrank up and literally fell through the grill into the coals.

But the worst part was Lake Wilco itself. I was the first to jump in. My wife Brenda followed me. The young people had better sense than we and were extremely hesitant. There was an area about the size of a large swimming pool bordered by lily pads. It was spring fed and cold as ice. But the worst part was the bottom. It was THE slimiest surface I have ever set foot in. Aaugh!!! I swam (feet off the bottom) over to my wife of six weeks and softly said, "Only for Jesus!"

In the 30 plus years since then there have been many, many, many (you get the idea) times when I have thought, "Only THROUGH Jesus." I have witnessed the same mind-set in many, other lives:

tragic accidents/deaths
marriage betrayals
loss of employment
teenage rebellion
surviving dysfunctional pastors
senior citizen limitations
personal moral failure
the death of personal dreams

In these and other painful passages of life I have lost track of the number of people who have not only demonstrated the strength of Christ in them, but who also have actually said, "I do not know how people get through this kind of thing without the Lord in their lives." Such comments almost always indicate a position of "when-I-am-weak-then-I-am-strong" testimonies. No brag, just fact. Paul's declaration is just such a testimony. Through Christ who strengthens us we can humbly yet assuredly say the same. The Christian walk is a Person-driven journey, enabled by the Presence who is with us always. Thanks be to God for his unspeakable gift!

Questions for Discussion

1. It is usually easier to see the sins of others than to see our own sins, particularly when our culture turns a blind eye to what it considers acceptable weaknesses or acceptable self-indulgence. What behaviors are acceptable to our society that run counter to the mind of Christ?

2. What is the difference between "Control yourself!" and "stir up the gift (of self control) that is within you"?

3. James 1:2-4 speaks of a process that leads to maturity. Why did the Creator make us this way rather than just zapping us with instant maturity?

4. Why is it important to see that God is like Jesus?

5. How was Jesus strong in becoming weak?

6. What difference does it make that Christ is always with us? How do we leverage that promise as a child of God?

7. How do you understand Paul's affirmation, "I can do all things through Christ who strengthens me"?

8. Why would Paul link knowing Jesus with the fellowship of Jesus' sufferings?

9. In John's gospel there are a variety of ways in which Jesus says, "Apart from the Father I can do nothing." Why would Jesus have emphasized his dependence on the Father?

10. Have you ever said or heard another person say, "I do not know how people get through this kind of thing without the Lord in their life"? What did you/they mean? How does this relate to doing all things through Christ?

CHAPTER THIRTEEN

With Hands Outstretched To Receive His Glorious Riches

Philippians 4:14-23

Yet it was good of you to share in my troubles. Moreover, as you Philippians know, in the early days of your acquaintance with the gospel, when I set out from Macedonia, not one church shared with me in the matter of giving and receiving, except you only; for even when I was in Thessalonica, you sent me aid again and again when I was in need. Not that I am looking for a gift, but I am looking for what may be credited to your account. I have received full payment and even more; I am amply supplied, now that I have received from Epaphroditus the gifts you sent. They are a fragrant offering, an acceptable sacrifice, pleasing to God. And my God will meet all your needs according to his glorious riches in Christ Jesus. To our God and Father be glory for ever and ever. Amen. Greet all the saints in Christ Jesus. The brothers who are with me send greetings. All the saint send you greetings, especially those who belong to Caesar's household. The grace of the Lord Jesus Christ be with your spirit. Amen.

Early in my years as a pastor I attended a denominational evangelism rally at Oral Roberts University. The speakers included Oral Roberts, Charles Allen and Luis Palau. Charles Allen was folksy in a glorious way. Luis Palau was riveting as he shared amazing stories of God's faithfulness. Oral Roberts did not resonate well with me. Sitting there in Tulsa amidst the evidence of his charisma, I could not deny his energy or extraordinary gifts, but the sermon he preached left me frustrated. Interestingly enough, I do not remember anything special the other preachers said, but I do remember the theme of Oral Roberts' message. Having described the poverty and humility of Jesus during the days of his incarnation, now that Jesus has been raised from the dead, Brother Roberts enthusiastically declared, "JESUS AIN'T POOR NO MORE!" The disconnect with that line of thinking was simple. It smacked too much of "prosperity theology," which no self-respecting-mainline-denomination, seminary-educated minister would ever regard with any attitude other than condescending scorn. Prosperity theology was a product of the exploding charismatic movement, which further marked it as questionable and even dangerous. My essential problem with that sermon was a concern that it was by-passing the call to discipleship—the call to take up one's cross, deny oneself and follow Jesus, to love God totally and one's neighbor as oneself.

The conservative Christian roots of my education taught me to mistrust the things of this world and fear the temptations of materialism. I was a subscriber to *Sojourners* magazine and frequently read *The Other Side*, both of which regularly chided middle-and upper-class American Christianity. Ron Sider's *Rich Christians in an Age of Hunger* had recently been a prophetic word to the prosperous church. I left that service feeling comfortably self-righteous.

Fret not. I got over it and in the decades since have endured the inescapable guilt that any prosperous person of conscience feels when comparing oneself to persecuted, starving, homeless, or simply underprivileged people around town and across the globe. So, how do prosperity-sensitive Christians handle the reality expressed by Paul at the end of Philippians when he refers to the *glorious riches* of God in Christ Jesus?

The Paradox of God's Prosperity In Christ

From an expository point of view, the idea of God giving out of the abundance of his riches can be contrasted to the limited resources from which the Philippians had given to Paul. He was encouraging the church to lean hard on God and to do so without fear of imposition. Paul could reasonably place limits on what he might ask of or expect from the church. They need not limit what they request of God simply on the basis of any concern over lack of resources.

These words encouraging trust in God sound exactly like what we would expect from a man who, as the letter began, said to his spiritual offspring, "I have you in my heart" (1:7).

I remember waving good-bye to our youngest daughter as she and her husband of three months set off to establish their first home 600 miles away. Back in the house my heart felt heavy as I looked into her room and saw the closet standing empty. Waving good-bye as their car drove away, she had seemed so fragile. I reminded myself that God would meet all their needs as they sought his will, and will do so far more profoundly than any earthly father could ever hope to do. There will be times when I will need to remind them of this, just as Paul reminded the congregation he loved.

Speaking of the gifts the Philippians had given to him, Paul compares their acts of assistance to a fragrant offering, an acceptable sacrifice. However, he prefaces it with an assurance that he is amply supplied. I expect Paul feared that, without meaning to do so, he might impose on the willingness of the Philippian church to sacrifice for his sake. Most of us like to be given gifts, but when such gifts are sacrificial they can be painful to receive. My family and I have known on more than one occasion what it was like to sit down to the table of a widow and feast out of her "mite." One such dear lady raised quail in her back yard, trying to scrape together a living. Serving us some of her *budddz* (birds), as she called them in her delightful drawl, was like dipping into her savings. It's been said that only the poor know the real meaning of hospitality. When such hospitality is received, it is deeply humbling and can be uncomfortable.

This is the kind of hospitality we receive at the Lord's table. "For you know the grace of the Lord Jesus Christ, that though he was rich, yet for your sakes he became poor, so that you through his poverty might become rich" (2 Cor. 8:9). *In what way do we become rich?* That's the question Paul raises in his concluding affirmation to the Philippians. How does the God who emptied himself and became a servant provide for us out of the riches of his poverty?

The Root of True Riches

Does this mean financial gain?

Occasionally, I do religious monologues and one of my favorite characters is blind Bartimaeus. That monologue is built around a theoretical pattern of thought in Bartimaeus' mind as he considers how to respond to Jesus' question, "What do you want me to do for you?" (Mark 10:51) The crux of this blind man's fear and trembling is this: Will the new privileges of being able to see outweigh the necessary adjustments and accompanying responsibilities?

"Can I handle being able to see?" this man born blind wonders.

As he ponders this dilemma, Bartimaeus hastily considers other things besides sight that he might ask of Jesus. An obvious suggestion many people would make to such an open question is to ask for money. He moves beyond that thought, but later realizes that if he had he made such a request, Jesus would not have been able to answer. Jesus essentially had no money.

Yes, Oral Roberts was right, Jesus ain't poor no more. But given the counsel of scripture as a whole ("thou shalt not covet" Ex. 20:17), the warnings of Jesus (Matt. 6:24, "you cannot serve God and money") and more particularly Paul's teaching on money (1 Tim. 6:10, "the love of money is the root of all kinds of evil"), it is unlikely that financial resources were fundamental to Paul's understanding of Christ's riches.

Jesus' encounter with the "rich young man" is instructive here (Matt. 19:16ff). This representative fellow is not only controlling with his worldly possessions, but he also wants to make *sure* he gets into heaven as well. Jesus, who came to set the captives free, advises him to move his investments from the bank to the lives of the poor. When the young man walks away disappointed in this prescription, Jesus then makes his proverbial comment about it being easier for a camel to pass through the eye of a needle than a rich man to enter the kingdom of God. What is he saying? He is saying that true riches are not a matter of what we control. *True riches are a matter of what controls us.* God's glorious riches in Christ Jesus are centered in what comes into our lives when we allow him—his love and truth—to be the controlling center of our lives.

Understanding God's New Math

When we think about the "daily bread" that God provides us, it is helpful to remember where that petition occurs in the Lord's Prayer. It comes between "Thy kingdom come, Thy will be done on earth as it is in heaven," and "lead us not into temptation." Both of these are directly related to the question of *what* is in charge of our lives.

I have no doubt that the request for bread, which Jesus also included, can be applied to physical needs. Martin Luther insisted that daily bread means "everything necessary to the support and comfort of existence, as food and raiment, house and land, money and goods, a kind spouse, good children, faithful servants, righteous magistrates, good weather, peace, health, honor, true friends, good neighbors and the like" (*The Lord's Prayers*, E. Trueblood, p. 53).

all your needs

Having acknowledged this application of the request for daily bread, it is instructive to take note of an episode that preceded Jesus' public ministry. In Matthew 4 we read of Jesus' temptations in the wilderness. Here was a living situation in which the issue of daily bread was cast into the crucible of temptation and questions of kingdoms and allegiances. It was in the heat of spiritual and physical struggle that Jesus quoted from Deuteronomy 8:3, "man does not live on bread alone." He was affirming that what we need daily in order to truly live is something beyond all the necessities in Martin Luther's list.

In the early chapters of another gospel, Jesus points to the heart of his Father's glorious riches. The disciples express concern that Jesus needs to eat and he replies, "I have food to eat that you know nothing about" (John 4:32). When his followers seem befuddled by that statement, Jesus continues, "My food is to do the will of him who sent me and to finish his work." The real life that Jesus came to bring—the glorious riches of God—is found in unity with God's will. A couple of chapters later, continuing to perplex the disciples, Jesus says that he himself is the bread of life and that those who come to him will never go hungry and never be thirsty (John 6:35). Is it not crystal clear that "the mind of Christ," which Paul in Philippians 2 enjoins us to emulate (the heart of this letter), is a state of surrender to the Father's will. In this submission is found glorious riches that no hunger or thirst can expel.

In a video follow up to the phenomenal best-seller *The Prayer of Jabez*, Bruce Wilkinson elaborates upon his understanding of this once-obscure prayer. I was gripped with a haunting sense of irony when near the end of the study he flatly stated, "Not many of us are going to learn how to release the hand of God through us." Amazing! Millions upon millions of people have read that book, but the author says most will not follow through on what they have learned. Why? Even God cannot expand our territory, as prayer asks, if we devote our lives to reinforcing fences where God is trying to put a gate. When we say "No" to God's will, we say "No" to his glorious riches.

God's new math seems foolish to the world, if not downright frightening, we gain our life (we expand our territory) by giving it up. Our temptation is to reverse the equation, we want to gain by gaining! Most of the millions who read *The Prayer of Jabez*, its author declares, will never embrace the math!

Like the wealthy young man drawn to Jesus, readers of *The Prayer of Jabez* sense something in it that can lead to a richer life. And like that young man, when it comes to letting God be in control and lead us out of our territory, we stop in our tracks and turn back. Our fears lead us to the temptation to hold back, which in turn prevents God's kingdom from taking shape.

I am amply supplied

Dietrich Bonhoeffer's famous statement, lived out in his own life, "When Christ calls a man he bids him come and die," is still a hard sell. But, the riches of God's grace in Christ Jesus give that call to self-denial a brilliant new meaning when we understand its power to bring life. God's riches in Christ Jesus are, in fact, his antidote to a spiritually lethal preoccupation with the bread this world has to offer. This truth is what enables the Lord to tell the church in Smyrna, "I know your afflictions and your poverty—yet you are rich!" (Rev. 2:9)

God Is Good All The Time—but We Can Use Some Help?

God is good. But, as Jesus was trying to make clear to the rich young man, we are not nearly so good as we like to think.

A pastor friend likes to use the formula, "God is good!" to which the congregation responds, "All the time!" to which he answers, "All the time," and they then respond, "God is good!" One day this friend was visiting a high school Sunday school class where the talk was about sex from a Christian perspective. During his remarks, seeking to mirror the attitude of the Bible, he said, "Sex is good." Before he could add another thought, a quick-thinking young man boomed out, "All the time!" A genuine confession of faith if one was ever made!

In *Too Busy Not to Pray*, Bill Hybels lists a string of what he terms "prayer busters." One of those is *selfishness*. It can keep us spiritually poor. In examining his own prayer life, he discovered that he had been praying, in effect, "Keep me from trial or tragedy or pain or anything that would make me really grow and become a man of God. Just give me a convenient, happy, satisfying problem-free life" (p. 92). That brings to mind the proverbial observation: Most people do not recognize opportunities because they come disguised as work. They come disguised as crosses, which feel like scary new territory. In Christ Jesus, God has new riches through which he can make clear the glory of our taking up our crosses, thus saving us from a self-serving, self-suffocating life.

God's riches in Christ Jesus are a new dimension of the same riches he revealed in the old covenant. Pardon the length, but a worshipful expression of them can be found in Psalm 103.

> Praise the LORD, O my soul;
> All my inmost being, praise his holy name.
> Praise the LORD, O my soul,
> And forget not all his benefits—
> who forgives all your sins
> And heals all your diseases,
> who redeems your life from the pit
> And crowns you with love and
> compassion,who satisfies your
> desires with good things
> So that your youth is renewed
> like the eagle's.
> The LORD works righteousness
> and justice for all the oppressed.
> He made known his ways to Moses,
> his deeds to the people of Israel:
> The LORD is compassionate and
> gracious,
> Slow to anger, abounding in steadfast love.
> He will not always accuse,
> Nor will he harbor his anger forever;
> he does not treat us as our sins
> deserve or repay us according to our
> iniquities.
> For as high as the heavens are above
> the earth,

so great is his love for those who
fear him;
as far as the east is from the west,
so far has he removed our
transgressions from us.
As a father has compassion on his
children,
so the Lord has compassion on those
who fear him;
for he knows how we are formed,
he remembers that we are dust.
As for man, his days are like grass,
he flourishes like a flower of the field;
the wind blows over it and it is gone,
and its place remembers it no more.
But from everlasting to everlasting
the Lord's love is with those who fear him,
and his righteousness with their
children's children—
with those who keep his covenant
and remember to obey his
precepts (1–18).

according to his glorious riches in Christ Jesus

The praise chorus "What a Mighty God We Serve" was true even
before Jesus brought us the gift of salvation. However, that does not
mean God did not need to do more to assist humankind to know
the glorious liberty of the children of God. A radically different act
of obedient faith was needed more fully to expose and unleash grace
and truth, to enable us to know the fellowship of God's sufferings
and resurrection power. When the Word became flesh and dwelt
among us (as described in Philippians 2; see also John 2:14), God
was offering the key to the vault that contained all of the riches

spoken of in scripture such as Psalm 103. This is a new and living way to receive God's riches that could be won only by the Messiah and can be experienced only by active faith in him.

What A Compassionate God We Serve

Think of the riches of his compassionate grace revealed so richly in the crucified flesh of Jesus, revealed in a servant's life. Maxie Dunnam retells a story from the practice of plastic surgeon Dr. Maxwell Maltz, author of the best-selling *Psycho-Cybernetics*, that offers a window on the riches of God's love as revealed in Jesus. A woman came to see Dr. Maltz concerning her husband. He had been badly burned attempting to rescue his parents from a burning house. The rescue attempt not only failed, but he was also left with a badly disfigured face and a deep burden of guilt for having failed to save his parents. He became a recluse, not wanting to be seen by anyone.

Dr. Maltz sought to comfort her with the assurance that advanced plastic surgery methods could restore her husband's appearance. She responded by explaining that her husband refused all help, having concluded that his disfigurement was God's punishment for the failed rescue attempt. Then she made a shocking request. "I want you to disfigure my face so that I can be like him. If I can share in his pain, then maybe he will let me back into his life. I love him so much; I want to be with him. And if that is what it takes, then that is what I want to do."

Of course, he would not agree, but her total love was deeply moving. He received her permission to try to talk with her husband. Going to the man's room, Dr. Maltz knocked persistently on the door. There was no answer. He called loudly through the door, "I know you are in there, and I know you can hear me, so I've come to tell you that my name is Dr. Maxwell Maltz. I'm a plastic surgeon, and I want you to know that I can restore your face."

There was still no response. After repeating the offer of help, Dr. Maltz finally told the man what his wife was requesting. "She wants me to disfigure her face, to make her face look like yours in the hope that you will let her back into your life. That's how much she loves you. That's how much she wants to help you!"

There was a brief moment of silence, and then, ever so slowly, the doorknob began to turn. The man came out to begin life again, compelled by his wife's gracious love (*This Is Christianity*, pp. 60–61). This remarkable story offers a glimpse of the rich love and grace of God in Christ Jesus.

Fleming Rutledge, noted Episcopal preacher, takes this one step further as she comments on words found in Psalm 22. They are given a whole new meaning when they come from the lips of Jesus who is on the cross: "My God, my God, why hast thou forsaken me" (Mark 15:34, KJV). As a backdrop she tells of a political prisoner in the small African nation of Guinea who had written on the wall of his windowless cell *in his own blood* (her italics) the words, "God save me." She notes, as she can so uniquely do, that Jesus' Cry of Dereliction is "the proving ground of our faith." With all the riches of God, we find times when no escape from the pain of the moment is possible. With amazement she observes that Jesus' death is not just his identification with the wretched of the earth, but it is even more. She affirms, "What we see and hear in Jesus' death is the decisive intervention of God to deliver his children from the unspeakable fate of ultimate abandonment." This was made possible, indeed was possible only, by his death (*The Undoing of Death*, pp. 13–15). Such riches could not have been known in their depth before the events of Holy Week.

Here God is tackling head on in his own blood that which gives him the worst public relations—the problem of evil and suffering. In Jesus, God is taking his own medicine, experiencing the unfairness and violence of life in which he calls us to continue to believe. This puts the riches of God in a whole different realm from the common image of an almighty God. As N. T. Wright says, "The Christian doctrine is all about *a different sort of God*—a God who was so different to normal expectations that he could, completely appropriately, become human in, and as, the man Jesus of Nazareth. To say that Jesus is in some sense God is of course to make a startling statement about Jesus. It is also to make a stupendous claim about God" (*Who Is Jesus*, p. 52).

"Deliver Us from Evil"–not Cheap Talk

Ravi Zacharias draws a startling conclusion from such insights by saying, ". . . God conquers *not in spite of the dark mystery of evil, but through it*" (*Jesus Among Other Gods*, p. 136). Philip Yancey writes much the same thing in the final chapter of *Reaching for the Invisible God*, where he concludes, "A relationship with God does not promise supernatural deliverance from hardship, but rather a supernatural use of it" (p. 283). The gifts of the Spirit and the fruit of the Spirit give us a surprisingly clear picture of the nature of the riches of God in Christ Jesus. Both enable children of God to be blessed in their ability to relate to God and neighbor as well as rich in the ability to serve God and neighbor. In his words on divorce found in Matthew 19:8, Jesus makes a telling observation about the spiritual poverty of the Hebrew people in the days of Moses, "Moses permitted you to divorce your wives because your hearts were hard." Modern Bible translator J. B. Phillips paraphrases it, ". . . because you knew so little about love." In Jesus Christ God has not only offered a profound picture of love, but by obedient love he has also conquered the principalities and powers whose influence helps keep human hearts hard.

The clearest snapshot of the principalities and powers at work in this generation took place on September 11, 2001. While it is probably dramatic to say that the world will never be the same again, such a statement is true for us who were alive when this horrific event took place. To this point I have avoided references to that day out of respect for all those lives directly touched by it, and out of a desire to avoid melodramatic use of an experience costly to so many. Here I make one exception, wanting to make as serious an application of the events as the events themselves.

I refer to that day because it puts us in touch with the intrinsic desire of evil to kill. In John 8:44 we hear Jesus say of the devil, "he was a murderer from the beginning." The hatred, the malice, the brutality, the viciousness, and the rage expressed when those four airplanes turned the towers, part of the Pentagon and flight 93 into fiery death traps, this quintessence of evil is nothing less than what evil sought to hurl at Jesus on that dark Friday. Jesus was the ultimate prize. Imagine, killing the Son of God!

But evil did not understand the full implication of the Son of God holding still in obedient faith while sin and death did its tortuous worst. Come Sunday morning the riches of God in Jesus Christ "appeared to Peter, and then to the Twelve. After that, he appeared to more than five hundred of the brothers at the same time. . . . Then he appeared to James, then to all the apostles, and last of all he appeared to me [Paul] also, as to one abnormally born" (1 Cor. 15: 5-8). Paul knew firsthand the amazing riches of God in Jesus Christ, riches that overcame the worst that evil could do.

At the end of the twentieth century, one of the most amazing evidences of these continuing riches began in the Bellavista prison in Colombia. This warehouse for terrorist assassins, where murder within the walls was a regular occurrence, became the gate of heaven. Hundreds of prisoners came to life-changing faith in Jesus Christ, transforming this foretaste of hell into a church. A college classmate of mine, Jeannine Brabon, has been a part of this miracle from its start. In her newsletter following 9-11, she included this report.

> At 10:30 a.m. I tuned into the radio program, "A CRY OF HOPE." Tears came as I listened to the brothers interceding for the U. S. acknowledging that they were once violent terrorists, but that God's love had been poured out into their lives. In another prison . . . three former terrorists who once hated the U.S. wept as they prayed for the disastrous evil unleashed upon innocent people.

Awesome! In Bellevista every day since January there is a prisoner who fasts and prays for President Bush. This is incredible in a country where many are hostile to the U .S., but this miracle takes place when the Love of GOD rules in a human heart.

If we see what God has done in Christ Jesus we fully understand that Jeannine used the correct word to describe what God in Jesus Christ had done—awesome!

The Lavish/Utterly Practical Riches of God's Grace in Christ

Let us not miss the heart of all of this. *Jesus never sought to be rich.* He sought to be faithful. Jesus warned about the *yeast* of the Pharisees and Sadducees, and in Mark 8:15, of Herod. Such is the yeast of those who, however subtly, want to be rich, who want to appear rich, materially or spiritually. Talk about irony. The yeast of the Pharisees won't rise! But the yeast of the mind of Christ is rich, full of resurrection life. It is when we give, not out of our abundance, but out of emptiness that we are the richest. Then we are giving by faith and not by sight.

At the heart of God's riches in Christ Jesus are the blessings Paul speaks of in Ephesians, saying, "In him we have redemption through his blood, the forgiveness of sins, in accordance with the riches of God's grace that he lavished on us with all wisdom and understanding . . . to bring all things in heaven and on earth together under one head, even Christ" (1:7-8, 10b). While sin is like centrifugal force, causing disintegration, the riches of God in Christ Jesus pull people and life together.

I was reminded of this power recently while reading the story of Christian apologist Josh McDowell's journey to faith in Jesus Christ. As a teenager he began searching for the answers to what are sometimes referred to as "first-order" questions: Who am I? Why am I here? Where am I going? His first approach to finding answers seemed logical enough. He jumped into church involvement

morning, noon and night. But rather than feeling better, he felt
worse. So he decided to chuck that in favor of higher education.
He made himself unpopular with the university faculty, always
asking another question and never being satisfied with the answers
he received. Still longing for purpose and meaning, he dived
into campus life, hoping that an activist reputation would bring
satisfaction within. It didn't.

In the midst of all his activity, he began to notice a small group
of students and faculty, 10 people altogether, who seemed truly
different. He saw in them both the courage of their convictions and
a loving spirit. His initial attempts at interaction with this group
were made problematic by the realization that these were "religious"
folks, and he had rejected that. Finally, he asked one of the young
women in this group what made them so different. Her answer
was direct, "Jesus Christ." At first he snorted in scorn, declaring in
no uncertain terms that he had rejected religion. She shot back, "I
didn't say religion. I said, 'Jesus Christ'." Then, to his surprise, he
was challenged to study the claim of Jesus to be God's Son.

When he realized how serious these people were, he determined
that he would do just what they were asking. His expectation,
however, was that he would have the satisfaction of proving them
wrong. He left the university and traveled throughout the United
States and Europe gathering "evidence" in the hope of writing a
book that would conclusively refute their claims about Jesus.

The result proved just the opposite. A growing sense of intellectual
dishonesty began gnawing at his gut. Finally, in spite of the fear
that becoming a Christian would be "ego shattering," one night in
Union City, Michigan, he prayed a prayer of confession, faith and
thanksgiving. Although there was no bolt of lightening, in the next
year and a half it became clear to him that he had experienced a
fundamental change from within.

The most significant change of direction in his life was in the area
of hatred and bitterness. One person in particular had been the
focus of this hatred. So deep was his anger that he could remember

lying in bed at night plotting how he could kill his father without being caught. His father was the town drunk.

In his formative years he lived in the constant shadow of shame and humiliation caused by his father's well-known behavior. Two months before his high school graduation he came home one day, greeted by the sound of his mother's sobs. "Son, your father has broken my heart. I have lost the will to live. All I want to do is live until you are graduated, then I want to die."

He was graduated two months later and the following Friday his mother died.

Five months after he prayed the prayer of salvation, he found himself looking his father in the eye, saying, "Dad, I love you." Clearly something had happened in his life.

Some time later, having transferred to Wheaton College, he was in a serious car accident. His father came to visit, remarkably enough, in a sober state. Josh confessed his years of hatred and affirmed the change of heart his faith in Jesus Christ had brought. His father answered, "Son, if God can do in my life what I've seen him do in yours, then I want to give him the opportunity." He then prayed a prayer of confession for all he had done and asked for faith to trust in Christ.

The change was immediate. After 40 years of drinking, he picked up a drink only one more time. Then he put it back down and knew he was free. Fourteen months later he died from complications related to the lifelong abuse of his body. But in that time the centrifugal force of sin was defeated. He experienced what Paul meant when he wrote, " . . . through Christ Jesus the law of the Spirit of life set me free from the law of sin and death" (Romans 8: 2). Both Josh and his father understood what it means to have your deepest needs met out of God's riches in Jesus Christ (*Why I Am a Christian*, ed. by N. Geisler & P. K. Hoffman, pp. 284-89).

The Joy Of The Lord (Who Emptied Himself) Is My Strength

The grace of the Lord Jesus Christ be with your spirit.

Hands of faith are outstretched hands. They long to be empty of the yeast of pride, reaching upward in the strength of faith made possible by God's grace. The joy for which Philippians is so well known is the paradoxical fruit of the mind of Christ in us. That mind is an attitude of trust in God accompanied by an intention to empty oneself of any designs on meaning outside of God's will.

At the end of *Mere Christianity*, C. S. Lewis echoes this attitude:

> But there must be a real giving up of the self. You must throw it away "blindly" so to speak. . . . The very first step is to try to forget about the self altogether. Your real, new self (which is Christ's and also yours, and yours just because it is His) will not come as long as you are looking for it. It will come when you are looking for Him. . . . The principle runs through all life from top to bottom. Give up yourself, and you will find your real self. Lose your life and you will find it. . . . Keep back nothing. Nothing that you have not given away will ever be really yours. Nothing in you that has not died will ever be raised from the dead. Look for yourself, and you will find in the long run only hatred, loneliness, despair, rage, ruin, and decay. But look for Christ and you will find Him, and with Him everything else thrown in (p. 190).

In the conclusion to *In the Name of Jesus*, Henri Nouwen writes,

> I leave you with the image of the leader with outstretched hands, who chooses a life of downward mobility. It is the image of the praying leader, the vulnerable leader, and the trusting leader. May that image fill your hearts with hope,

courage, and confidence as you anticipate the new century (pp. 92–93).

God in Christ Jesus stretched out his hands to us and held nothing back. As a result, we can do the same to him in return.

A fellow pastor became father to a daughter born with spina bifida, a condition in which a portion of the spinal cord is exposed at birth. Across the years of the child's life she endured several surgeries. Each one was more dreaded. Into her elementary school years, it became apparent that another operation was needed. She was old enough to resist, but her parents knew they had to press on. The day of the surgery she was very afraid and agitated. Her father walked beside her bed as she was rolled toward the operating room. All the way she pleaded to go back home. Finally, they arrived at the door where the father could go no further. He watched the doors swing behind her bed as it rolled through the doors. Suddenly everything became still. Her pleading abruptly stopped. In a clear voice she called out, "I love you, Daddy." All the way to those doors she had cried, "Why have you forsaken me?" But in the moment of truth she knew she was anything but forsaken. She was rich.

"And my God will meet all your needs according to his glorious riches in Christ Jesus."

Let us stretch our hands out in faith to the God who in Jesus Christ can make us rich in all the ways that really matter.

To our God and Father be glory for ever and ever. Amen.

Questions for Discussion

1. What does the statement "only the poor know the real meaning of hospitality" mean to you? Have you ever experienced such hospitality?

2. Assuming we do not live by bread alone, what do we live by?

3. If God's will is so enriching, why do we resist it?

4. What helps us take up difficult crosses when resurrections feel so far away?

5. What does Jesus add to the riches already found in the old covenant?

6. What does the Maxwell Maltz story illustrate in relation to what God in Christ Jesus has done?

7. If Jesus was God-forsaken so that nothing could separate us from his love, what does this add to Psalm 103?

8. Why were Josh McDowell and his father rich? How did they get that way?

9. How do we "give ourselves up"? Why does this bring freedom?

10. Are your hands outstretched, empty of pride and fear, ready to say "Yes" to God's call in Jesus Christ?

Bibliography

Books

Abraham, William J. *Waking from Doctrinal Amnesia*. Nashville: Abingdon Press, 1995.

Barnes, Craig. *When God Interrupts*. Downers Grove: InterVarsity, 1996.

Barnes, Craig M. *Sacred Thirst*. Grand Rapids: Zondervan, 2001.

Bennis, Warren. *On Becoming a Leader*. Reading, Massachusetts: Addison-Wesley Publishing, 1989.

Boggs, William. *Sin Boldly: But Trust God More Boldly Still*. Nashville: Abingdon Press, 1990.

Bonhoeffer, Dietrich. *The Cost of Discipleship*. New York: Macmillan, 1959.

Borg, Marcus. *The God We Never Knew: Beyond Dogmatic Religion to a More Authentic Contemporary Faith*. New York: Harper Collins, 1997.

Bruce, F.F. *Paul: Apostle of the Heart Set Free*. Grand Rapids: Eerdmans, 1977.

Buckingham, Jamie. *The Last Word*. Plainfield, NJ: Logos International, 1978.

Cailliet, Emile. *Journey Into Light*. Grand Rapids: Zondervan, 1968.

Campolo, Tony. *How to Be Pentecostal Without Speaking in Tongues,* Dallas: Word. 1991.

Campolo, Anthony. *Who Switched the Price Tags?* Waco: Word Books, 1986.

Chambers, Oswald. *My Utmost For His Highest, Updated Edition in Today's Language.* Grand Rapids: Discovery House, 1992.

Cloud, Henry and Townsend, John. *False Assumptions.* Grand Rapids: Zondervan, 1994.

Covey, Stephen R. *Principle-Centered Leadership.* New York: Fireside, 1990.

Covey, Stephen R.. *The Seven Habits of Highly Effective People.* New York: Fireside, 1990.

Craddock, Fred. *Interpretation: A Bible Commentary for Teaching and Preaching.* "Philippians." Atlanta: John Knox Press, 1985.

Dostoevsky, Fyodor. *The Brothers Karamazov.* Translated by Andrew R. MacAndrew. New York: Bantam, 1981.

Dunnam, Maxie. *This Is Christianity.* Nashville: Abingdon, 1998.

Fitzgerald, Earnest. *Keeping Pace: Inspirations in the Air.* Greensboro: Pace Communications, 1988.

Foster, Richard. *Freedom of Simplicity.* New York: Harper Paperbacks, 1981.

Geisler, N.L. and Hoffman, P.K., eds. *Why I Am a Christian.* Grand Rapids: Baker, 2001.

Glasser, William. *Take Effective Control of Your Life*. New York: Harper & Row, 1984.

Guinness, Os. *The Call*. Nashville: Word Publishing, 1998.

Hamilton, J. Wallace. *Still the Trumpet Sounds*. Old Tappan, NJ: Fleming H. Revell Company, 1970.

Hansel, Tim. *When I Relax I Feel Guilty*. Elgin, Il.: David C. Cook, 1979.

Horney, Karen. *Neurosis and Human Growth*. New York: W.W. Norton & Company, 1950.

Hybels, Bill. *Too Busy Not to Pray*. Downers Grove: InterVarsity, 1988.

Jones, E. Stanley. *Conversion*. Nashville: Abingdon Press, 1959.

Kelly, Thomas. *A Testament of Devotion*. New York: Harper & Row, 1941.

Kinlaw, Dennis. *Preaching in the Spirit*. Grand Rapids: Francis Asbury Press, 1985.

Kinlaw, Dennis. *The Wesleyan Bible Commentary*, Charles W. Carter, general editor, *Vol. II*, "Song of Solomon". Grand Rapids: Eerdmans Publishing, 1968.

Lebow, Barbara. *A Shayna Maidel*. New York: Dramatists Play Service, 1988.

Lewis, C.S. *Mere Christianity*. London: Collins, 1952.

Lewis, C.S. *Surprised By Joy: The Shape of My Early Life.* Orlando: Harcourt Brace & Company, 1955.

Luccock. Halford. *The Interpreters Bible,* George A. Buttrick, commentary editor. *Vol. VII,* "Mark". Nashville: Abingdon Press, 1951.

Marshall, Katherine (ed.) & Peter. *Mr. Jones Meet the Master.* Old Tappan, NJ: Fleming H Revell, 1950.

Mason, Mike. *Practicing the Presence of People.* Colorado Springs: WaterBrook Press, 1999.

Mason, Mike. *The Gospel According to Job.* Wheaton: Crossway Books, 1994.

Miller, Keith. *The Becomers.* Waco: Word Books, 1973.

Miller, J. Keith. *The Secret Life of the Soul.* Nashville: Broadman & Holman Publishers, 1997.

Nouwen, Henri. *In the Name of Jesus.* New York: Crossroad, 1993.

Osborne, Cecil. *The Art of Understanding Yourself.* Grand Rapids: Zondervan, 1967.

Osborne, Cecil. *You're in Charge.* Waco: Word Books, 1973.

Packer, J.I. *Knowing God.* Downers Grove: InterVarsity Press, 1973.

Peck. M. Scott. *The Road Less Traveled.* New York: Simon & Schuster, 1978.

Peck, M. Scott. *The Road Less Traveled and Beyond.*. New York: Simon & Schuster, 1997.

Phillips, J.B. *The New Testament in Modern English.* New York: Macmillan, 1958.

Phillips, J.B. *Your God Is Too Small.* New York: Macmillan, 1961.

Pippert, Rebecca Manley. *Hope Has Its Reasons.* San Francisco: Harper & Row, 1989.

Putnam, Roy. *Getting It All Together.* Nashville: Abingdon Press, 1977.

Rutledge, Fleming. *Help My Unbelief.* Grand Rapids: Eerdmans, 2000.

Rutledge, Fleming. *The Undoing of Death.* Grand Rapids: Eerdmans, 2002.

Schaef, Anne Wilson. *Co-dependence.* San Francisco: Harper & Row, 1986.

Schaeffer, Francis A. *True Spirituality.* Carol Stream, IL: Tyndale House, 1972.

Seamands, David. *Healing for Damaged Emotions.* Wheaton: Victor Books, 1988.

Seamands, David. *Healing of Memories.* Wheaton: Victor Books, 1985.

Shoemaker, Helen Smith. *I Stand By the Door.* Waco: Word Books, 1967.

Sjogren, Steve. *Conspiracy of Kindness.* Ann Arbor: Servant Publications, 1993.

Slaughter, Michael. *Spiritual Entrepreneurs.* Nashville: Abingdon Press, 1994.

Solzynetzin, Aleksandr. *The Gulag Archapelago 1918-1956: An Experiment In Literary Investigation.* New York: Harper & Row, 1973.

Spock, Benjamin. *The Common Sense Book of Baby and Child Care.* New York: Duell, Sloan & Pierce, 1946.

Stedman, Ray. *Spiritual Warfare.* Grand Rapids: Discovery House, 1999.

Stott, John R. W. *Guard the Gospel.* Downers Grove: InterVarsity Press, 1973.

Sweet, Leonard I. *Quantum Spirituality.* Dayton: Whaleprints, 1991.

Swindoll, Charles R. *Encourage Me.* Grand Rapids: Zondervan, 1993.

Swindoll, Charles R. *Living Above the Level of Mediocrity.* Waco: Word, 1987.

Tournier, Paul. *The Meaning of Persons.* New York: Harper & Row, 1957.

Tozer, A.W. *The Knowledge of the Holy.* New York: Harper & Row, 1957.

Trueblood, Elton. *The Lord's Prayers*. New York: Harper & Row, 1965

Twain, Mark. *Life on the Mississippi*. Montreal: Dawson Brothers, 1883.

Watson, Philip S. *The Message of the Wesleys*. Grand Rapids: Francis Asbury Press, 1984.

Weatherhead, Leslie D. *The Transforming Friendship*. Nashville: Abingdon Press, 1977.

Wheelis, Alan. *How People Change*. New York: Harper & Row, 1973.

Whitney, Donald. *Spiritual Disciplines for the Christian Life*. Colorado Springs: Nav Press, 1991.

Wiersbe, Warren W. *Be Joyful*. Wheaton: Victor Books, 1974.

Wilkinson, Bruce. *The Prayer of Jabez*. Sisters, Oregon: Multnomah Publishers, 2000.

Wills, Dick. *Waking to God's Dream*. Nashville: Abingdon Press, 1999.

Wright, N.T. *The Challenge of Jesus*. Downers Grove: InterVarsity, 1999.

Wright, N.T. *Who Was Jesus?* Grand Rapids: Eerdmans, 1992.

Yancey, Philip. *Disappointment With God*. Grand Rapids: Zondervan, 1988.

Yancey, Philip. *Finding God in Unexpected Places*. Nashville: Moorings, 1995.

Yancey, Philip. *The Jesus I Never Knew*. Grand Rapids: Zondervan, 1995.

Yancey, Philip. *Reaching for the Invisible God*. Grand Rapids: Zondervan, 2000.

Yancey, Philip. *Soul Survivor*. New York: Doubleday, 2001.

Yancey, Philip. *What's So Amazing About Grace*. Grand Rapids: Zondervan, 1997.

Yancey, Philip. *Where Is God When It Hurts*. Grand Rapids: Zondervan, 1977.

Zacharias, Ravi. *A Shattered Visage*. Grand Rapids: Baker. 1990.

Zacharias, Ravi. *Can Man Live Without God*. Dallas: Word, 1994.

Zacharias, Ravi. *Cries of the Heart*. Nashville: Word, 1998.

Zacharias, Ravi. *Deliver Us From Evil*. Dallas: Word, 1996.

Zacharias, Ravi. *Jesus Among Other Gods*. Nashville: Word, 2000.

Articles

Arn, Wynn. "Closing the Evangelistic Back Door." *Leadership*, Vol. V, No. 2 (Spring, 1984): 24-31.

Cunneen, Sally. "Abundant Life." *Leadership*, Vol VII, No. 3. (Summer 1986): 38.

Kenner, Craig. "Mutual Mahem." *Christianity Today*. Vol. 48, No. 11 (Nov. '04): 60-64.

Liston, Tim. Cartoon. *Leadership*, Vol. XVII, No 4. (Fall, 1996): p. 101.

Miller, Dennis. "Gentle Discipline." *Leadership,* Vol VI, No. 2, (Spring, 1985): 69.

Moyers, Bill. "Let's Get Jesus Back." *The United Methodist Reporter,* Vol. 151, No. 48 (April 8, 2005): 4a-5a.

Petti, Michael. "God's Pursuit." *Leadership*, Vol VII, No. 3. (Summer, 1986): 39.

Robbins, Duffy. "Youth Ministry in Adolescence: Mistaking Cynicism For Discernment." *Good News*, Vol. 38, No.4. (Jan/Feb, 2005): p. 29.

Willard, Dallas. "Spiritual Formation in Christ For the Whole Life and the Whole Person." *Vocatio*, Vol 12, No. 2. 4-7.

Zwingelberg, Chris T. "Sin's Peril." *Leadership,* Vol VIII, No. 1. (Winter, 1987): p. 41.

Praise for With Hands Outstretched

"It has been a special spiritual treat for me to read *With Hands Outstretched*. When I finished I felt I had experienced some special time with John Wesley. It is classic Wesleyan teaching. I'm sure I speak for Salvationists everywhere of our gratitude for his skillful handling in making the doctrines we share shine so beautifully. This is a sparkling work and I recommend this book with joy to saints, sinners and seekers at every level of development."
Commissioner Andy Miller, Sr., *National Commander, The Salvation Army, retired*

"I picked up this book and simply could not put it down. If I could choose only one study book to share with a congregation, this would be it. It is filled with poignant quotes, clear workable illustrations and great spiritual depth. This author shares profound truths which could greatly transform any church from declining to dynamic. If this book does not light your fire, then your wood is wet."
Dr. Rose Sims, *author of* New Life For Dying Churches

"Through the years Don Adams has shared with me his thoughts and feelings as he strives to be the person God intended him to be. He is open, honest and articulate. His message will give you great encouragement in your journey."
Bill Turner, Chairman, Executive Committee, Synovus; *author of* The Learning of Love—A Journey Toward Servant Leadership

"In his powerful book, *With Hands Outstretched*, Dr. Adams has "broken the vase" and the fragrance of his faith, his wisdom and his pastor's heart fill our nostrils... and surely the nostrils of God.

"Through Dr. Adams' *With Hands Outstretched* I encountered the Apostle Paul and Jesus Christ. Through his amazing use of images, I gained greater understanding of the "Letter to the Philippians." The further I delved into the book, the more I was praying... with hands outstretched!

"Dr. Don Adams, in his thoughtful and challenging commentary on "The Letter to the Philippians," gives us vivid images that give us spiritual eyes to see and ears to hear Paul's timeless messages!"

Rev. Greg McGarvey, Senior Pastor, *Carmel United Methodist Church, Carmel, Indiana*